Blake Chapman

OCEAN ANIMALS

THE WEIRDEST, SMARTEST AND SNEAKIEST SEA CREATURES

Illustrated by
Astred Hicks

CSIRO
PUBLISHING

For my amazing little animals, Hannah and Boston.
I love you to the bottom of the deepest ocean, through all of the
swirling-whirling currents, and back! – BC

Text: © Blake Chapman 2020
Illustrations: © Astred Hicks 2020

A catalogue record for this book is available from the National Library of Australia.

ISBN: 9781486311415 (pbk)
ISBN: 9781486311422 (epdf)

Published by:
CSIRO Publishing
Locked Bag 10
Clayton South VIC 3169
Australia

Telephone: +61 3 9545 8400
Email: publishing.sales@csiro.au
Website: www.publish.csiro.au

Edited by Sally McInnes
Cover, internal design and typesetting by Astred Hicks, Design Cherry
Printed in China by Toppan Leefung Printing Limited

Feb20_01

Contents

ACKNOWLEDGMENTS

I would very graciously like to thank and acknowledge the wonderful team at CSIRO Publishing for all of their help, support and guidance on this book. In particular, I'd like to thank Lauren Webb for her endless patience with me and very clever and helpful feedback.

Many thanks to my extremely talented friends and colleagues who provided their incredible photographs for use in the book! If you ever need some inspiration on loving (or photographing) marine animals, definitely head to their web pages and scan through their photos: Denice Askebrink, Simon Pierce (@simonjpierce; https://oceantripper.com), Ailie Suzuki and Tamzin Henderson (https://www.tamzinnz.com/). Also, a huge thanks to the absolute rock stars who read draft chapters of this book and provided fantastic feedback: Anna, Adeline Perreca, Alden Perreca, and Harry S-H.

And lastly, but most of all, I'd like to thank Clint Chapman for his unwavering support of me and everything I do. Thank you for your ideas and inspiration, and for discussing material for the book with me – whatever time of the day (or night) it might have been. But most of all, thank you for just being you. My favourite marine moments are the ones we've shared!

Marvellous marine animals

A GLIMPSE INTO MARINE LIFE

If you visit a beach and look closely, you'll get a tantalising glimpse into the array of life that is found in the oceans. You'll probably notice sea birds first. They can be loud and obvious as they run around, seemingly playing tag with the surf. Some of these birds may have travelled thousands of kilometres to end up on that beach! While scanning the sand, you might find shells, cuttlebones (the hard, internal structure of cuttlefish) and tangles of seagrass that have washed up with the waves. Looking out to sea, you could be lucky enough to catch sight of various mega marine mammals, such as dolphins or whales.

You'll probably see a lot of things you can't identify, too. For example, a big blob of something that, if you're honest with yourself, looks a lot like a puddle of snot! Look – but don't touch it! It could be a jellyfish! Even a piece of a dead jellyfish's tentacle can still hurt you with one of its thousands of stinging cells. These cells shoot harpoon-like barbs

that inject deadly venom into predators or prey. The jellyfish sting is one of the fastest movements in nature, too – it all happens in less than one-millionth of a second!

Or, this blob could be something else, entirely. If it doesn't have tentacles, but instead has lots of tiny little dots inside, it might not be *an* animal at all. Instead, it could be moon snail eggs. Phew, harmless. But still interesting! Moon snails are really cool little animals. They eat by drilling their tooth-covered-tongue-like structure, called a radula, through the shells of other animals, while injecting acid at the same time! Moon snail eggs are laid in a jelly substance that absorbs sea water and swells into a transparent horseshoe-shaped goo-sausage.

These incredible coastal animals are just a tiny snapshot of the living things that depend on the ocean. Marine animals come in every size, colour and shape imaginable; this book will introduce you to lots of these. But it will also introduce you to some animals that will require you to believe in the unimaginable, too!

As you read, you will find some words written in **bold**. These super-scientific words are defined in the Glossary at the back of the book.

WHAT ARE MARINE ANIMALS?

Marine animals are reliant on the oceans or marine **ecosystems** for some or all aspects of their existence. Crucially, they also all have ways of coping with lots of salt! Aside from those things, though, there is no other rule about what a marine animal is. Most marine animals filter oxygen out of the water to breathe, but some breathe air directly from the **atmosphere**. Many marine animals swim, but some – for example, crabs – walk just as **terrestrial** (land) animals do. Also, like terrestrial animals, some marine animals have skeletons, while others don't.

Nothing quite signifies the sometimes-bizarre diversity of life in the oceans like hammerhead sharks. They certainly are magnificent – but they have such an unusual and unlikely head shape!

SIMON J PIERCE

THE WORLD OF MARINE ANIMALS

Our oceans are like nothing else. Literally! Earth is the only planet known to have liquid water on its surface. Not only do we have water, but we have *lots* of water: around 71% of our planet is covered by oceans. The main difference between marine water and fresh water is salt. It is estimated that in the 1370 million cubic kilometres of water in the oceans, there are 50 quadrillion (or 50 million billion) tonnes of salt!

Marine environments are ... wet. I doubt this comes as a surprise to you. But marine environments are different to terrestrial environments in other ways, too. Two other examples are temperature and light. Ocean temperature is usually quite stable, whereas air temperature can change quickly, and it varies over a wider range (very hot to very cold). Natural light is almost always available on land, to some degree at least. However, most of the ocean is completely dark, with light from the sun, moon and stars only reaching into the shallow depths.

Within the oceans, there are many different **habitats**. These range from bustling coral reefs, rocky shores and kelp forests to lonely **abyssal** plains, deep-sea **trenches** and **seamounts**, and the expansive open ocean, or **pelagic** zones, in between.

Coral reefs, formed by colonies of coral polyps, are the most diverse of all marine ecosystems. Although they cover just 2% of the oceans' floors, up to a whopping 25% of all marine **organisms** rely on these reefs. In contrast, the open ocean is very sparsely populated, and animals often need to travel long distances to find food or a mate.

Deep depths

The deepest known point in the Earth's oceans is found in the Mariana Trench in the western Pacific Ocean, where the seafloor dips down more than 10.5 kilometres!

MARINE HABITATS

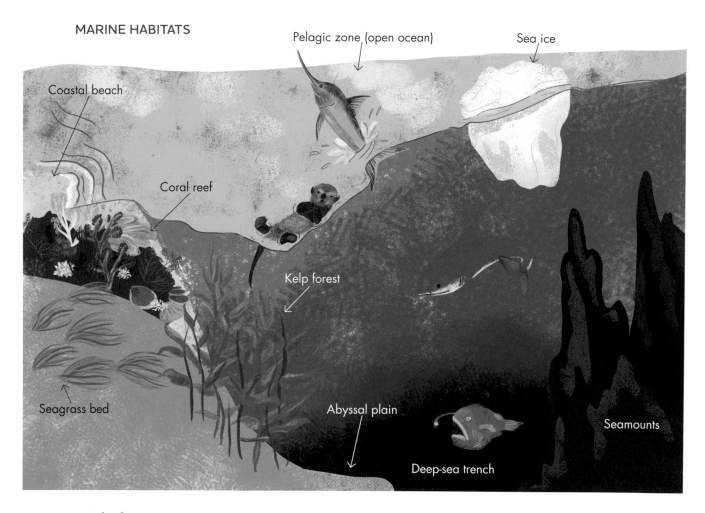

Pelagic zone (open ocean)

Sea ice

Coastal beach

Coral reef

Kelp forest

Seagrass bed

Abyssal plain

Deep-sea trench

Seamounts

Kelp forests are interesting and unique ocean ecosystems favoured by many animals, such as sea otters. Although kelp looks like a plant, it is actually a type of extremely large brown algae. Some kelp can grow to over 50 metres high (all underwater), and by as much as 60 centimetres in a single day! Built-in bubble-like air bladders keep the kelp afloat, helping the flexible algae grow towards the water's surface, where the sunshine is brightest. Kelp forests are also some of the most dynamic marine environments – that is, they can change rapidly, including appearing and disappearing!

Coral reefs support an enormous diversity of life.

Kelp forests are a magical sight, and they support lots of marine life!

There are also completely bizarre marine environments, such as deep-sea hydrothermal vents. Hydrothermal vents are openings in the sea floor that spew out superheated water (up to 400°C!) and a concoction of chemicals nasty enough to be toxic to most living things. Yet, some hardy marine animals call hydrothermal vents home-sweet-hot-salty-home!

WHAT'S IN THIS BOOK

Each chapter of this book has a feature of marine animals as its theme. This could be something that helps the animals to survive and thrive, or something that makes them unique or extra-incredible. You will learn about underwater defence, creatures that are huge and those that hide, and animals that seem like they couldn't possibly be real. You'll also read about animals that use high speeds or ocean currents, those that can be deadly to humans, and others that cooperate with each other or are just really smart! The chapters also include species profiles, which provide extra detail about particular animals. Make sure to check out the web resources that are suggested throughout the text, too – just be sure to check with your parents before you do so.

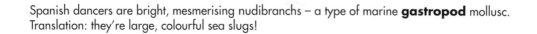

Spanish dancers are bright, mesmerising nudibranchs – a type of marine **gastropod** mollusc. Translation: they're large, colourful sea slugs!

Some of the critical issues currently threatening marine life are also discussed. But luckily, a variety of ways that *you*, as well as your friends, family and classmates, can help are also provided.

A brief introduction to taxonomy, or how animals are scientifically grouped through shared characteristics, is found at the end of the book.

Whether you're a fan of fish, a connoisseur of **crustaceans**, mad about **molluscs** or mammals, in wonder of worms, or if you seek out sea birds, rave about reptiles or just love jellyfish, this book has got you covered!

Masters of defence

ARMED AND DANGEROUS

Imagine you're walking along the sand, gazing into the shallow pools of water created by the surrounding **fringing reef**. You see a beautiful shell! So, you reach down and grab it. But instead of scoring a great treasure, you get a very nasty, very painful shock. And before you know what's even hit you, your hand and arm have gone numb. This is the result of a **toxin** that is so complex, chemists have still not been able to develop an effective antivenom (a treatment to reverse the effects of a **venom**). You've disturbed one of the world's most venomous snails: a cone snail. The cone snail was obviously not trying to eat you – you're enormous! Instead, it was just trying to defend itself against a potential threat. After all, you did get very close.

Beware! Cone snail shells may look like beautiful treasures but touching them is a bad idea! There could be an animal inside that is extremely venomous.

Cone snails are some of nature's most impressive chemists. They make two types of venom. One is used to defend themselves against **predators** or big creatures that could harm them (like you!), while the other type is used for hunting **prey**. The venom used for defence is 350 times stronger than the venom used for hunting, which makes sense if you think about it – snail predators are usually much bigger than snail prey! Cone snail venom is made up of more than 100 000 different components. When the snails see a tasty worm, for example, they mix just the right components together to make a hunting venom. But if a predator is lurking nearby, they use a different recipe to produce a defence venom instead. Genius!

Healthy hint

Cone snail shells come in many sizes, colours and patterns, and they can be really tempting to pick up. But the best advice when you're in a marine environment is *'if it's a cone, leave it alone!'*

There is safety in numbers, so these fish 'school' together.

VENOM, POISON OR TOXIN?

Venoms and **poisons** are both forms of biological toxins produced by animals. The notable difference between the two is how they are delivered. Venoms have to be injected through a bite or sting; they need an entry point to get into the bloodstream. Poisons, on the other hand, get into the body by being swallowed, inhaled or absorbed through the skin. Venomous animals, like sea snakes, jellyfish and stingrays, are often more active in defending themselves; whereas poisonous animals are often more laid-back, letting their reputation precede them. Some animals – like the blue-ringed octopus – can be both venomous and poisonous! Yikes! Seems a bit over*kill* to me!

JUST PUFFERING 'A-ROUND'

Marine environments can be scary places. No matter what you are, there is almost always another animal that is bigger than you, and it often wants to eat you! Marine animals need to be able to defend themselves, and they have some extraordinary ways of doing this. Some animals use venom to hurt potential predators. Others use **camouflage** or special tricks to hide or escape from threats. Some fish 'school' – or swim together in large groups – for protection. In this formation, individual fish would be harder for a predator to focus on. When tightly grouped together, the school could also look like a much larger object, which would be more intimidating to potential predators. Then, there are those animals that opt to stand their ground and fight ... or at least defend themselves.

Some animals, like this stingray, hide by burying themselves in the sand.

One of the funniest defence strategies is the one used by pufferfish. Pufferfish are able to rapidly inflate their bodies by quickly gulping large amounts of water into their extendable stomachs. They expand so much that their skin stretches, causing small spines (that are usually flattened against their bodies) to stick out. These fish can inflate in as little as 15 seconds. The final outcome is a spiny, floating ball, three or four times its original size, with comically small fins. So, not only does the fish grow into a far larger animal than a would-be predator originally thought, but it also suddenly 'grows' its own weapons! This defence strategy would surely deter all but the largest and most determined predators!

Predators often find they have tried to bite off more than they can chew with pufferfish … these fish can quickly turn from a small bite-sized snack into more than a mouthful!

While inflated, pufferfish are so puffy that they can't swim as well as usual. Eventually, they expel the excess water, but it can take more than five and a half hours for the fish to deflate to their normal size.

As if the ability to blow up into a spikey ball was not enough, pufferfish also contain tetrodotoxin (TTX), one of the most potent biological toxins currently known. Interestingly, this toxin is used not only for defence but also as a chemical signal that females use to attract males. Even baby pufferfish have a small amount of TTX on their body surface to deter mini-puffer predators. However, some predators have developed **adaptations** that allow them to be safe from the toxic effects of TTX.

Pufferfish defend themselves through 'non-evasive defence' strategies. This means that they don't actually run (or swim!) away from a predator. Looking at their bodies and their clumsy swimming pattern even when 'deflated', you can tell these fish are not built for speed. Instead of having a streamlined body shape, they are round and

What are you looking at?! Haven't you seen an inflated fish before?

Puffy art

Male pufferfish use their body and fins to build large, beautifully patterned nest pits on the ocean floor to attract mates. Look up 'pufferfish nest' online to see some of the impressive designs. Females choose their mate partly based on their attraction to his pit design. After the females deposit their eggs, the males remain in the centre of the nest for 6 days to care for them.

stout with very small fins. Since they can't out-swim their predators, they defend themselves by putting on a big, scary appearance and producing a toxin that makes most predators very sick – all while staying still. Animals that use non-evasive defence strategies need to continue to defend themselves until predators lose interest and decide to find something else to eat.

Even when deflated, pufferfish give off a slick 'don't eat me!' vibe!

Sea-lebrities
FLOWER URCHIN

BERNARD DUPONT

Flower urchin toxin comes out of the sweet-looking 'petals', not the spines! In fact, the spines in this species aren't even sharp!

Sea urchins are **echinoderm** (Eee-ky-no-derm) **invertebrates** related to starfish, brittle stars and sea cucumbers. They often have long, movable, brittle spines that can easily break off when disturbed. These bizarre little animals have 'tube feet' that they use to move, catch food and hold onto the ocean floor. Their mouth is located on the underside of their body and contains a five-point, star-shaped jaw, which they use to scrape algae and other foods from rocks.

Although flower urchins sound lovely, these pretty pink animals have spines and miniature pincer-like limbs with movable jaws that they hide within their 'blooms'. They also contain a potent toxin that can cause paralysis and death to a variety of species. The scientific name for flower urchins, *Toxopneustes pileolus*, which translates to 'poison breath skull cap', is no exaggeration!

Flower urchins wander the floors of coral reefs, seagrass beds and rocky or sandy environments, and they like to 'dress' themselves with pieces of dead coral or other debris. It's not entirely understood why they do this, but they are often almost completely covered. They might be using the coral to help weigh themselves down or to stabilise themselves in moving water. Or, they could be using the coral like a hat to provide shade from the sun. Could these be the most sun-smart marine animals?

Some people consider the internal fleshy bits of sea urchins to be an excellent form of healthy protein and a culinary delicacy. So next time you don't feel like steak, fish or beans, you might consider urchin! Did I mention, though, that the parts you eat are actually the animals' reproductive organs! As a result of the demand for these tasty delights, sea urchins are heavily fished in some areas.

NOW YOU SEE ME, NOW YOU DON'T!

Squid are incredible animals that have evolved a number of superhero-like defence mechanisms. Like their close mollusc relatives, octopuses and cuttlefish, squid can change their colour, pattern and shape to match their surroundings. They can also use water jets to speedily propel themselves away from danger, and evasive swimming movements to out-manoeuvre predators. And when those things are not good enough, they bring out the big guns … and squirt ink!

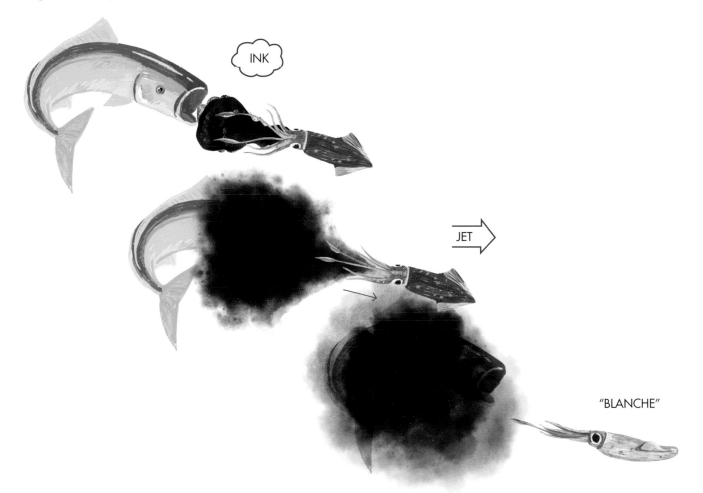

Ink is one of the most fascinating defence tactics used by squid. In fact, they can actually squirt a blob of mucousy ink that holds a squid-like shape in the water! They can also produce a cloud of ink that disperses over a larger area, providing a magician's cloak-like screen for them to disappear behind. What makes this strategy *even better* is that the chemicals in squid ink send a signal to other squid that there is danger in the area. These same chemicals may also block smell and taste receptors in predators, causing them to abandon their pursuit!

Inky animals

The ability of animals to produce ink is so cool! It is also really rare. It seems that only some cephalopods, like squid, octopuses, cuttlefish – but not nautiluses – and sea hares, which are funky gastropods that look like (sometimes regurgitated) leaves of lettuce, have this ability. Sea hares use ink as a chemical defence weapon and repellent. Their ink is purple!

Squid will often use a combination of their abilities to escape predators. One of the most popular combinations is the 'ink-blanche-jet manoeuvre'. This consists of the squid ejecting ink, turning itself white (blanching), and quickly squirting water to jet away.

SLIPPERY SCAVENGERS

When talking about defence, who could go past the awesomeness of slime? That's right ... slime. So, let's talk about hagfish! Hagfish are little-known, eel-shaped fish that live at the bottom of deep-sea environments in the arctic seas and the north Atlantic and Pacific oceans. A few different species of hagfish exist, and they are all very strange!

Hagfish have been referred to as 'the slimy sea creatures of your nightmares'. Why, you might be wondering? Their skull is made of cartilage, they have five hearts, no jaws and no stomach. They have eyespots, but these very basic forms of eyes are most likely only capable of detecting light, not seeing images as we do. Hagfish skin, which contains nearly a third of their blood, is loosely fitted to their bodies. They don't have paired fins (those that appear on both sides of the body). Instead, they have a single fold of skin that runs along the top and bottom of the 'tail'. They also have a single nostril and six to eight barbels, which are bizarre whisker-like organs around their mouth. So basically, they are not very attractive. And, considering that hagfish live in groups of up to 15 000 individuals, maybe they are a bit nightmarish!

This hagfish is putting its best face forward for the camera. Really!

Hagfish are the ultimate scavengers. They literally dive headfirst into their meal — burying themselves into whatever yummy rotting animal carcass they can find and drilling right into the middle of it. They then eat away at the carcass from the inside out! Hagfish are so 'into' their food that by being fully enclosed within it, they can absorb its **nutrients** directly through their skin!

But there is more to hagfish than meets the eye. These animals have gone down the 'yuck' path in not only their appearance but also for their defence strategy: slime! Slime is used for a variety of purposes in nature, but most commonly for helping things to move and for creating stickiness. Hagfish, however, have taken slime to a whole new level! They produce a concentrated mucus-based slime that oozes from small pores on their body. Inside the hagfish, the slime ingredients are kept coiled up

Sea-lebrities

SEA SNAKES

Sea snakes are some of the most common and venomous reptiles in the world. Luckily, they use their venom mostly for catching a meal rather than as a defence. Most sea snakes are not aggressive, only using their one to three pairs of short fangs to bite if they are provoked. However, a few species, like the olive sea snake and ornate reef sea snake, are known to be a bit more aggressive. Serious **envenomation** to humans occurs in around 20% of bites, and death in about 3%.

Sea snakes range in length from just over 1 metre to a very intimidating 3 metres. They have flattened, rudder-like tails that they use for swimming. Most sea snakes live in the warm coastal or reef environments of the Pacific and Indian oceans, but the yellow-bellied sea snake prefers the open ocean. Because of this specialised distribution, climate change could present a ssslippery ssslope for this sssspecies.

CHRISTIAN GLOOR

Sea snake fangs are just like needles: long, thin and hollow, with a sharp point at the end.

CHRISTIAN GLOOR

Sea snakes, like this banded sea krait, often have unmissable body colours and patterns, broadcasting to any potential predator that they are not to be messed with.

tightly in microscopic bubbles called mucin vesicles. But as soon as they are released into the sea water, the vesicles swell and burst, releasing invisible threads of protein and other slime components. These uncoil, mix, and bind large quantities of sea water together – a process that is a bit similar to you making jelly from a box mix. And just like that, the area is *filled* with sticky slime. The hagfish slime production process is so quick that it is not only effective against predators that bite, but also against lightning-fast suction feeders, like certain species of sharks. The whole process takes place in just a fraction of a second. Amazingly, despite its thick, sticky form, the final hagfish slime product is 99.996% water!

INSIDE THE SLIME

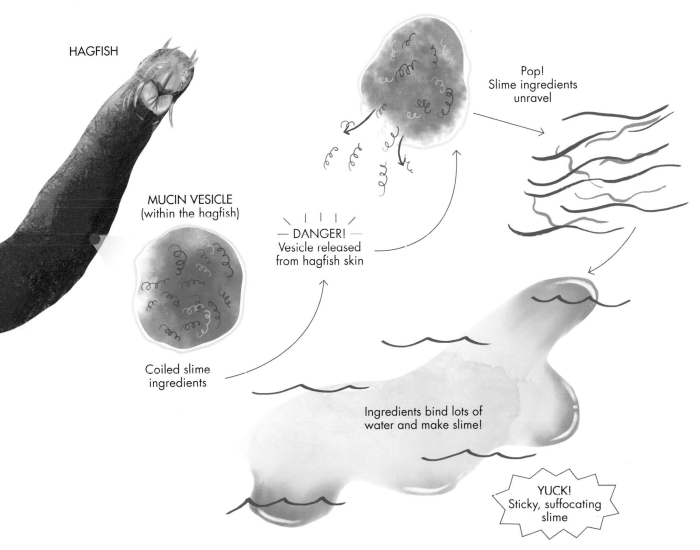

HAGFISH

MUCIN VESICLE
(within the hagfish)

Coiled slime
ingredients

— DANGER! —
Vesicle released
from hagfish skin

Pop!
Slime ingredients
unravel

Ingredients bind lots of
water and make slime!

YUCK!
Sticky, suffocating
slime

But besides being an icky-sticky surprise, how does slime protect hagfish from wanna-be predators? After all, it is so hard to catch prey in the large, open expanses of the deep sea, that marine predators are not easily turned off by something that is just a bit yucky. Instead, slime deters predators by choking them! Fish extract oxygen from the water using their gills. If their gills get slimed, then they can't breathe. This is obviously a big problem! A slimed, suffocating predator is much more focused on trying to breathe than eat so usually swims away to clear its goo-covered gills. It is unlikely to bother a hagfish again any time soon after an experience like that!

Hagfish have a strange but effective way of protecting themselves from their own slime. They cleverly tie themselves into a tight sliding knot, momentarily forming a pretzel shape. In this way, they use their own bodies to strip off and escape from their slime. What's even more incredible is that the specific motions the hagfish go through while 'knotting' themselves also break the slime apart, allowing it simply to wash away. These animals clearly have all the right moves!

Oversized underwater

Elephants are enormous, giraffes are giant, dinosaurs were daunting, and hippopotamuses are humongous! But, the biggest land animal, the African elephant, weighs in at a measly 6300 kilograms. The tallest of the tall giraffes measure just 5 metres, Brachiosaurus stood at only 13 metres tall (we think), and Supersaurus had a neck possibly up to 15 metres long. Hippos weigh a puny 4000 kilograms. Well, 'measly', 'just', 'only' and 'puny' if you're a blue whale, that is!

Blue whales may be able to reach lengths of 30 metres, but animals this big would be very rare and unusual. A more realistic measurement of the largest of large individuals is around 25 metres. This is roughly equivalent to half the length of an Olympic swimming pool, about twice the height of a Brachiosaurus, or the length of three fire trucks parked one behind the next. It would take four elephants in a line to equal the length of a blue whale and many, many more to equal the weight! It's pretty neat to think that blue whales – which are thought to be the largest animals to have *ever* lived – are swimming around in our oceans right now!

HOW BIG IS BIG?

It is hard to determine exactly how big really big
animals are. Can you imagine trying to weigh a
whale? Where would you even find a scale that big!
And despite their bulk, some really big animals are
also really fast – blue whales, for example, can out-
swim sail-powered boats! Other super-sized marine
animals live in places that can be very difficult for us
to get to. As a result, they can be extremely hard to
study. Occasionally, these giant animals wash up on
beaches, giving us a better view of their ginormous
bodies. But because they were likely sick, injured,

When it comes
to animals, the
blue whale is the
biggest of big!

Exploding blubber bombs

Occasionally, when whales die, they wash ashore. After a mammal dies, its body continues to change. The bacteria that work so hard to break down the body produce a brew of stinky gasses as they go. If these gasses put too much pressure on the decaying whale's skin, the whale can become a massive blubber (and guts) bomb. When this happens, bits of rotting whale can splatter nearly half a kilometre! This is a super-smelly, super-gross, super-sized problem!

or just plain old before they washed up, they are often smaller than their healthy relatives. On the other hand, people often like to exaggerate the size of things. When you tell all your friends about the amazing sea giant you found, you might just add on a metre … or five!

As a result of the difficulty in weighing and measuring healthy giant animals, a lot of myths have been passed around. For example, you might have heard that the heart of a blue whale is the size of a car or that you could swim through its blood vessels. A dead 23.3-metre-long blue whale washed ashore not too long ago. This was sad, but it gave scientists an incredible opportunity to test some of these theories. They were able to learn that blue whale hearts, while certainly massive, at around 1.5 cubic metres and 180 kilograms, are actually much smaller than a car. Also, a human would not be able to swim through its blood vessels – a medium-sized fish, like a salmon, probably could though! Although not as big as they were rumoured to be, blue whales' hearts are still about 14 times heavier than those of African elephants and 640 times as heavy as yours. They can pump 220 litres of blood per beat!

Sea-lebrities
ELEPHANT SEALS

TAMZIN HENDERSON

'What did you call me?!?' How adorable are these elephant seal weaners among a colony of king penguins!

There are two species of elephant seals: northern elephant seals, which are found in the north-eastern Pacific Ocean, and southern elephant seals, which are found in the sub-Antarctic and Antarctic oceans. The big nose of male elephant seals (which is called a proboscis) looks somewhat like an elephant's trunk, giving these animals their name. The proboscis can be used to make a roaring racket. But interestingly, the large surface area of the nose also helps the seal to reabsorb moisture that they breathe out while they are on land for extended periods – like during the mating season!

Southern elephant seals are particularly massive – they are even bigger than polar bears! Why so big? The bigger the seal, the deeper they can dive during fishing trips and the more fat they can store. Male elephant seals use their large bodies to fight each other to gain the loyalty of females. Size matters for females, too. Females need to tip the scales at 300 kilograms before they can have babies and they will not have a male baby until they hit the 380-kilogram mark!

As true seals (meaning they have no external ears and smaller, more streamlined limbs), elephant seals are great in the water! Northern elephant seals can reach speeds of over 8 kilometres per hour during dives. Other **pinnipeds**, such as sea lions and fur seals, have small external ears and larger, more flexible flippers, which instead are a big help on land! They are called eared seals.

WHAT A GUTS!

Blue whales, along with their baleen whale relatives, filter their food out of the water. Surprisingly, the favourite food of these giants is teeny-tiny **plankton**. It is pretty cool to think that such large animals can survive on such small food, especially since it takes a lot of energy for such big creatures to swim. But it seems like this love of miniature food is exactly what allows them to grow so big. Even though planktonic organisms are small in size, they exist in huge numbers. It is lucky they do because blue whales are eating machines! Estimates of blue whales' food intake suggest that they may eat up to 3.6 metric tonnes of krill *every day*. It's a good thing they also have extra-large mouths! The massive need to feed means that these hefty animals can only live in parts of the ocean that are highly productive. In this case, 'productive' means that the ocean conditions are just right for the growth of organisms that form the bottom of the marine **food chain**, like plankton. These parts of the ocean are teeming with life since food is plentiful.

A lot of theories exist on how and why gigantic animals evolved. The most obvious reason is that the bigger you are, the less of you will fit into a hungry predator's

HOW TO EAT TEENY-TINY FOOD: THE BLUE WHALE MOUTH

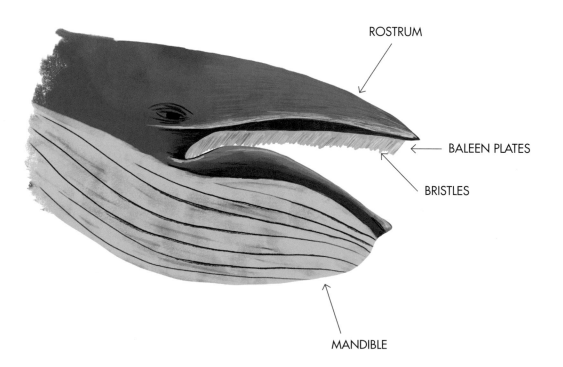

ROSTRUM

BALEEN PLATES

BRISTLES

MANDIBLE

Plankton comes in all shapes because it includes lots and lots of different plant and animal species.

Krill is one of the most important types of plankton for our extra-large marine animals.

mouth. While that makes sense, in the case of blue whales, the reason is probably less violent. It is likely that during certain periods in the distant past (such as the Pliocene, Palaeocene and Eocene), ocean conditions were perfect for plankton growth. More plankton meant more food, and this allowed animals to become bigger.

As ocean temperature, acidity and currents change because of climate change, the amount and location of plankton will also change. Because blue whales and many other small, medium and extra-large marine animals rely on plankton to survive, less plankton in the oceans could be a problem of epic proportions!

Whale sharks are the biggest fish in the sea, but they are gentle giants.

SIZE MATTERS

The largest *fish* in the ocean, the whale shark, can grow as large as 20 metres long and weigh around 34 tonnes. However, whale sharks typically seen in today's oceans are rarely over 10 metres. Despite their size and brilliant colour and pattern, these animals are experts at the game of hide-and-seek! Adult whale sharks are difficult to find, so there could still be bigger ones out there. Like blue whales, whale sharks, as well as basking sharks and megamouth sharks, are **filter feeders**!

Sharks, including whale sharks, are chondrichthyans, or cartilaginous fish – meaning their skeletons are made of cartilage, not bone. The longest 'teleost', or *bony fish*, is the oarfish. Oarfish have a maximum length of 8 metres, but more commonly they only reach lengths of 5 metres. That is still a big fish! Although oarfish are the longest bony fish, ocean sunfish are the heaviest. One sunfish that measured

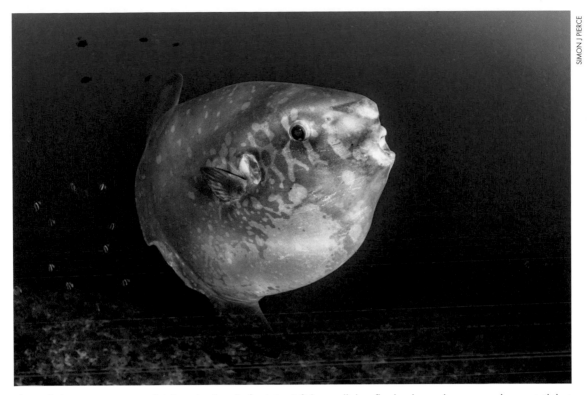

The truly bizarre ocean sunfish has the head of a (giant) fish, a tall, but flat body, and a stumpy, lumpy tail that often looks like it was patched on as an afterthought!

3.3 metres long and 3.2 metres tall weighed in at 2300 kilograms! This animal had died and washed ashore: when alive and healthy, it probably would have weighed even more!

There are even ginormous jellyfish! Nomura's jellyfish are thought to be the most massive by weight. The bells of these giant jellies can reach 2 metres in diameter (that's longer than your bed!), and they can weigh up to 200 kilograms. Although Nomura's jellyfish can give off a nasty sting, their sticky, stingy tentacles are not the longest in the oceans – that honour is reserved for the lion's mane jellyfish. Because lion's mane jellyfish tentacles are so fine and dense, they can easily break. As a result, it's not known exactly how long they can grow, but lengths of somewhere up to *30 metres* are considered possible. Longer tentacles would allow for more prey-catching capability. However, long tentacles – like long hair – can become tangled. Tangled tentacles would be highly problematic since this would make it more difficult for the jelly to get prey to its mouth.

Sea-lebrities
GIANT TUBE WORM

Giant tube worms are not only huge but also hugely unusual! Their tube homes, which are made of chitin (pronounced ky-tin) – the same substance that is used to make crab shells, squid beaks and fish scales – can be 3 metres tall. The worm itself, which can weigh in at a whopping 650 grams, is about a metre shorter than its home. Most of the worm stays inside the tube; however, it sticks the very top part of its body out of the 5-centimetre hole at the tip of the tube. This feathery-looking bit of the worm is called the plume and it is bright red because it is filled with blood.

Giant tube worms have a strange idea of the perfect place to call home: they live around deep-sea hydrothermal vents! Luckily, their tube protects them from the toxic nasties that pour out of the vents.

Giant tube worms don't have a mouth or stomach. Instead of wasting energy on pesky things like eating and digesting, they employ billions of bacteria to do it for them. These bizarre bacteria live in the tube worm's body, and they do all the hard work in terms of producing energy. Giant tube worm bacteria are special – they can turn gas into sugar! The worm's plume catches the gassy goodness from the vents. The gasses are then passed through the worm's blood to the bacteria. And *BAM*! Homemade worm food!

COLOSSAL CRUSTACEANS

On the floor of the Pacific Ocean near Japan, giant crabs tiptoe around, scavenging meals. Japanese spider crabs can have leg spans of 3.7 metres (that's longer than two human adults laying head-to-toe!) and weigh over 13 kilograms. Crab shells are great armour, but unfortunately, they aren't very roomy and don't allow for growth. As crabs outgrow their shells, they have to shimmy out of the old one before they can grow a new one. Not only do they have to get their body, head and eyes out of the shell but also each of their long, long legs! If the crab gets stuck during this process, its legs could become deformed – or even worse, it could die! Talk about growing pains! This process of shedding the shell is called **moulting**, and it can take hours, or even more, to complete.

BLAKE CHAPMAN

Have you ever gotten your head stuck while trying to get your jumper off? If so, spare a thought for this moulting Japanese spider crab!

Out-of-this-world big

Although not the biggest of animals, exactly, the Great Barrier Reef (GBR) is the biggest living structure on Earth. It is made up of 3000 individual reefs and stretches for 2000 kilometres! The GBR is teeming with life, which stems from a base of billions of coral polyps. The GBR is the only living organism that can be seen from space.

By the time the crab gets its old shell, or **exoskeleton**, off, it already has a new shell – but it is extremely soft. Without its toughest line of defence, the crab is easy prey for hungry predators until the new shell hardens; this can take around 7 days. There is safety in numbers, though, and some species, like the bright orange giant spider crab, come together in the thousands to all **moult** at the same time.

Marine isopods are strange deep-sea scavenging crustaceans related to the roly-poly bugs you sometimes find under a rock on land. Most land, freshwater and marine isopods are teeny-tiny little things. But some marine species are giant – they can grow as big as 50 centimetres long! Like something out of a scary movie, they have been reported to swarm the carcasses of dead animals that sink to the ocean depths.

Why do creatures like Japanese crabs and deep-sea isopods get so big? Scientists don't really know, but it is possible that the cold water at the bottom of the sea helps animals to grow bigger and live longer. Animals might also strive to grow larger so that they can store more fat to help them through times when food is scarce.

NOAA OKEANOS EXPLORER PROGRAM, GULF OF MEXICO 2012 EXPEDITION

Marine isopods can grow to be huge and abundant in some deep ocean environments.

Fantastical creatures

FACT, OR FANTASTICALLY FICTITIOUS?

Beautiful mermaids would call to sailors with their songs, and the terrible kraken could drag a whole ship underwater with its humongous tentacles. That is, at least, according to legend. But these creatures might not have been entirely 'fanta-sea'. Instead of beautiful half-woman, half-fish creatures, the original mermaids were most likely actually sea cows (like dugongs and manatees) seen by sailors in need of a very long, land-based holiday!

SIMON J PIERCE

Is this a mermaid? A cow? No, it's a manatee!

Sea-lebrities
DUGONG

MARK GOODCHILD

Dugongs spend their days mowing through the seagrass.

BERND.NEESER/SHUTTERSTOCK

What is not to love about these beautiful, round, sirens-of-the-sea?

Dugongs, along with their manatee cousins, make up the group affectionately known as sea cows. These lovable, rotund grey-brown marine mammals with big snouts and curious whiskers can grow to more than 3 metres in length and live for 70 years or more! The scientific name of their **order** is 'Sirenia', which was taken from the name for mermaids in Greek mythology: sirens. Up until about 250 years ago, there was another, much larger sea cow called the Steller's sea cow. Unfortunately, these animals were hunted to **extinction** shortly after they were discovered in the 1700s.

Dugongs are true **herbivores**, and they are considered to be seagrass community specialists. You can often tell if dugongs have been in an area by the tell-tale feeding trails they leave through seagrass meadows. Post-dugong, these areas pretty much look like someone has taken a lawnmower straight through! If conditions are good, and dugongs feel safe, they feed by 'excavating' seagrass. This means they eat the whole plant – the underground roots and all! When they don't feel as safe, they just mow off the tops. The whole plant gives them a lot more value for effort, but excavating leaves them more exposed to predators, such as tiger sharks, because digging clouds the water and makes it difficult to keep watch for threats.

Dugongs cleverly keep track of major changes to their food supply and environment. If conditions are not right, they will hold off on having babies until things improve.

And the kraken that attacked ships, drowning or even eating the unfortunate crew? Well, that big guy was probably a larger-than-life giant squid. The sea would have been a scary place for early sailors, so making up stories and characters to explain the dangers could have been a way that the sailors dealt with their fears. And of course, these stories made the sailors sound really tough, too!

While Greek mythology catches our attention with centaurs, which are half-man, half-horse, and satyrs, which are half-goat, half-man, the oceans provide us with real-life animal combos! Sawfish, for example, have the rear of a ray (which is a type of fish) and the snout of a saw! Although they look awkward, sawfishes' saws are extremely important and powerful sensory devices. By waving their saw back and forth over the ocean floor (like a metal detector), they can locate prey, even if it's buried. Even better, they can wave their saws through the water like a ninja to hit, slice, pin down or impale prey!

Sawfish are just what their name says: saw in the front, fish in the back.

THEY WANT TO SUCK YOUR BLOOD

Although they have a really cool name, vampire squid don't live up to the legend of their blood-sucking mythical namesakes. Instead, the sea lamprey is the true Dracula of the water world. Lampreys are ectoparasitic fish, which means that they target the outside of prey to feed on. Like the slimy hagfish mentioned on p. 22, lampreys look like eels and don't have bones or jaws. But they still have a really scary mouth! Lamprey mouths open out to form a wide, round sucking plate covered in sharp, horn-shaped teeth, which they use to latch onto their prey. They then use their tiny-tooth-covered tongue to carve through their prey's scales and skin so that they can slurp on the unlucky animal's blood, body fluids and tissue. Uuggghhhh! The feeding style of lampreys is so destructive that they kill as many as six out of every seven animals they suck onto. They are not picky, either; a wide variety of fish and marine mammals are victims to their 'sucky' ways. Sea lampreys have even been seen stuck to basking sharks – the world's second-largest fish, and one that is heavily defended by tough scales!

Sea lampreys are native to the Atlantic Ocean, but they have both marine and freshwater parts to their life cycle. They move into inland freshwater rivers and streams to find a mate, build a nest and then ... *bite other fish, causing them to become blood-sucking sea lampreys too*! Just kidding on the last part: that honour is reserved for the vampires of legend. Instead, sea lampreys make baby lampreys by the far less fantastical pathway of laying eggs. But, they can lay up to 100 000 of them! Then, having done their job, the adults – who purposefully stopped eating to put every last bit of their energy into producing their babies – pretty much shrivel up from the inside out, and die! It's kind of sweet and heroic ... for parasitic bloodsuckers!

Baby lampreys are so different to their parents. They are born with no eyes and no teeth, and they eat by filtering tiny organisms and sludge out of the water. Baby

Ewww, spit!

Bizarrely, like garlic to a vampire, sea lampreys are repulsed by the smell of human spit!

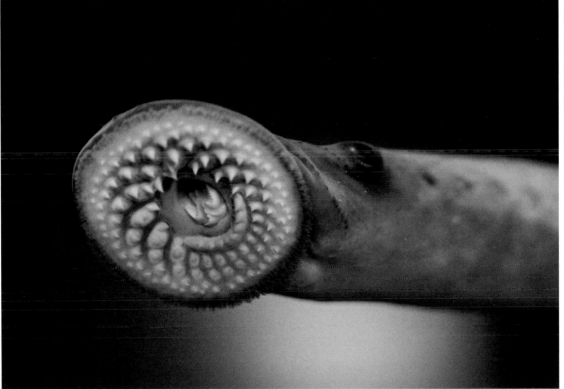

Are sea lampreys really the stuff of nightmares, or just nightmarishly cool? You decide!

lampreys live in the soft sediment of the streams where they were born for as long as 7 years. Then, as if actually bitten by a vampire, they go through a dramatic, life-altering transformation. They grow some eyes, a freaky mouth full of teeth, move to the ocean, suck an animal's body fluids, and decide that's the life for them! Until, that is, they decide to have babies of their own, at which time they go back to freshwater environments, mature further, stop eating, and, well, you know the rest ...

OHHH, SHINY!

Magic is one of the key elements in fantasies. And like sparks being shot out of a wizard's wand, some animals can produce magical displays of light. Light that is produced by living things is called **bioluminescence**. Sparkly, shiny bioluminescence in the ocean can provide a brilliant show, even if it takes the form of vomit. Wait; what? Yes, you read that correctly – one species of deep-sea shrimp uses bioluminescence to *vomit* light! Life in the ocean can be so magical.

Light can be hard to come by in the ocean, especially in the deep sea. Therefore, bioluminescence can be very handy. Because it's so useful, at least 1500 species of fish alone use bioluminescence! Some animals chemically concoct their own light, whereas other animals encourage teeny-tiny light-producing organisms to jump on board and then share their light.

But what is bioluminescence actually used for, you might be wondering? If your grumbling tummy woke you up in the middle of the night, and you wanted to get a midnight snack, what would you do? First things first, you're going to need some light. You might turn on a torch or flick a light switch to help you find your way to the biscuits in the kitchen. Some marine animals use the same strategy to locate food in their own dark environment.

Bioluminescence, looking like blue sparks at the water's edge here, can make the sea shimmer, shine and light up in all sorts of unbelievable ways!

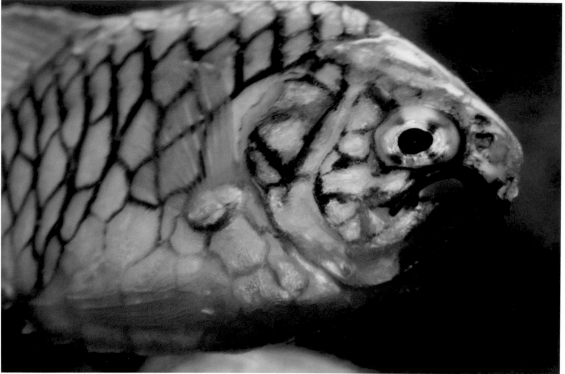

Pineapple fish have a symbiotic arrangement with luminescent bacteria, which gives the fish built-in headlights (although, they are really just light organs on the lower jaw). The bacteria are always 'on', so for 'lights out' the fish simply closes its mouth, hiding the bacteria.

Even better, bioluminescence can also be used to lure food straight to a hungry mouth – no navigating through the dark on your own required! Light is highly interesting and exciting in the dark ocean, so animals become curious around it. But ... it should be explored with caution! After all, investigating a light could result in you having a chunk taken out of you by a cookiecutter shark, or lead you straight into the enormous fangs of a viperfish! Cookiecutter sharks light up their bellies, which results in curious animals coming to check them out. When a prey-worthy animal comes close, they suck on, insert their teeth (sort of like lampreys do), spin around, and leave with a perfect cookiecutter-like cut-out of flesh. No guesses needed on how they got their unusual name! The cookiecutter shark's strategy is so efficient that they are known to feed on quick and highly capable prey, such as whales, other sharks, seals, and even tuna!

Viperfish, on the other hand, dangle a light from the end of a long, stalk-like fin in front of their mouth, flash it on, and then wait patiently for something to come and check out the strange floating light. And when they do ... chomp!

That's a no-brainer!

A viperfish's fang-like teeth are so long that they have to stick out from the jaw. If they were kept inside the mouth, they would poke straight through into the fish's brain.

Interestingly, bioluminescence can even be used to *protect* an animal from a hungry predator. This brings us back to our favourite deep-sea shrimp. When being chased, the shrimp can vomit a bioluminescent substance. This may temporarily distract or blind predators, giving the shrimp an opportunity to furiously flip out of the danger zone.

Other animals, like the Atolla jellyfish, use light as an emergency scream for help. Once caught by a predator, there is often not much hope left. However, this jellyfish (and certain other species) can light up in a display known as a 'burglar alarm' in the hope of attracting an even larger predator. You may think it seems a bit silly to try to *attract* large predators, but the idea is that the presence of the larger predator may scare the smaller predator enough to, well, 'lose its lunch'. Not quite in the same way as the vomiting shrimp though ...

When it comes to casting spells, snapping shrimp would even triumph over Harry Potter in 'Stupefying' things. But in the shrimp's case, no wand is needed! Instead,

Going, going ... gone

Unfortunately, some marine species are threatening to perform the worst kind of magic – the disappearing act. They are disappearing from the oceans entirely. But unlike in magic tricks, they do not come back. As of 2017, the International Union for Conservation of Nature (IUCN) determined that 65 species of fish (that we know of) had become 'extinct'. A further 87 species were 'possibly extinct', and six more were considered to be 'extinct in the wild' (with living representatives of these species only surviving in aquariums). Another 362 fish species were 'critically endangered', which means they are very close to extinction. The critically endangered and possibly extinct species accounted for a whopping 3% of all fish species investigated. We need to take urgent action to prevent these amazing marine animals from disappearing for good!

they use their oversized 'snapper claw' to produce a killer bubble. While bubbles certainly don't sound threatening, these special super-fast, ultra-loud, really hot and bright bubbles are so powerful that they can stun or even kill small animals in their path. How cool is that! The bubble-casting shrimp can then drag its stupefied prize back to its burrow to feast.

Search '*Atolla wyvillei* video' and 'Amazing pistol shrimp stun gun' online for some great video footage of these animals in action!

SMITHSONIAN ENVIRONMENTAL RESEARCH CENTER

Snapping shrimp are just one of the many species known to use bioluminescence.

WHAT DO YOU WANT TO BE WHEN YOU GROW UP?

Have you ever bitten your tongue? It hurts, right? But it could be worse! Meet the tongue biters. These small isopods are marine **parasites**. They drift in the ocean until they bump into a fish. Then they jump on, head straight for the tongue, hook on with their seven pairs of legs and don't let go. They cut off the blood supply to the fish's tongue and slowly suck out the remaining blood. Eventually, the tongue shrivels up and falls off. The parasite then – get this – takes the place of the tongue. That's right ... the tongue biter snuggles into the fish's mouth, gets nice and comfy-cosy, and lives out the rest of its life as a false tongue.

Let's just stop here for a moment and take a second to fully appreciate what's happening here. The *parasite* takes the place of the fish's *tongue*!

I wish I was making that up!

Some tongue-biter parasites – yes, there are *dozens* of species of these miniature monsters – have even lost the function of their eyes. That's probably a good thing because let's 'face' it, a tongue with eyes is just weird! Seriously – check out the photo to 'see' for yourself!

What makes these bizarre little biters even more interesting is that they all start out as males. The first tongue biter to stake its claim on a fish not only takes the place of the tongue, but it also changes into a female. However, if a tongue biter lands on a fish that already has another tongue-biter parasite on it, he misses out on his destiny of becoming a tongue. Instead, he stays as a male and usually settles down on the fish's gills.

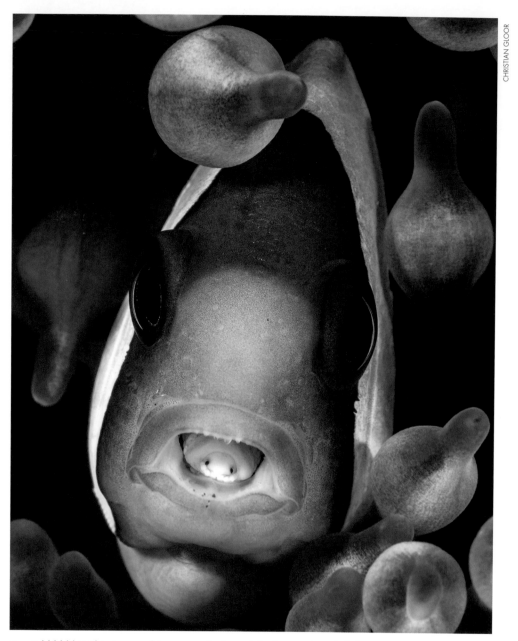

CHRISTIAN GLOOR

Say 'ahhhhhh'! This tongue-biter parasite is no joke for its clownfish host.

A female tongue-biter parasite can lay up to 100 eggs at a time, while still carrying out her tongue duties. She'll keep the eggs in a pouch on her abdomen where they'll go through two, or sometimes more, moults before reaching juvenile status. That's right – the poor fish has to try to eat and get on with its normal business while 100 baby parasites moult away in its mouth: twice! After the moults, the young parasites are released into the water, driven to become a tongue one day themselves!

The need for speed

V8 Supercars reach top speeds of close to 300 kilometres per hour, and Usain Bolt has clocked a top speed of over 12 metres per second. In these cases, speed is for sport. But for marine animals, the need for speed is often to eat or to avoid being eaten! Speed can also be used in unexpected ways – for example, to generate the power to smash!

However, animals (including human animals) rarely use their maximum speeds. Think about how fast you can move, then think about how often you *actually* move that fast. With the exception of running a race, it is probably not that often! Why? Well, moving fast has a lot of downsides. First of all, it's harder to do and it uses a lot more energy. Moving fast also reduces the amount of control you have over your movements. And finally, the faster you move, the less aware you are of your surroundings. So, although moving fast might be an option, it is generally not the best option. Even in a life-threatening situation – like avoiding a predator – the 'need for speed' needs to be balanced with the ability to function in other ways too.

SWIFT SLASHING SWORDS

Billfish, which include swordfish, spearfish, sailfish and marlins, are considered to be the fastest fish in the ocean. These are sleek, normal-looking fish – until you see their heads! They have a long sword in the place of where you might instead expect to see a nose. This 'bill' is called a **rostrum**, and it is an extension of the fish's top jaw.

The fastest billfish have been estimated to reach top speeds of 130 kilometres per hour. However, this is probably an overestimate. Instead, it is more likely that these fish can reach top speeds of around 50 kilometres per hour. Also, they only swim at these speedy-speeds a small percentage of the time. In fact, they usually swim quite slowly.

Surprisingly, billfish don't even appear to use their top gear to catch prey. Although they are extremely fast swimmers, they are also quite big. There are differences between the species, but adult billfish can reach a whopping 4 metres in length. Their prey, such as sardines, anchovies and squid, can't swim as fast as billfish can. However, they are smaller and more agile, so they can dart away from big, hungry mouths. To counter the manoeuvres of their prey, billfish use swift movements of their awesome rostrum to help them hunt.

One extra-speedy billfish is the sailfish, named for its large sail-like **dorsal fin** (which looks a bit like a mohawk!). When hunting, sailfish will casually swim up behind a school of fish – sardines, for example – ever so slowly. They then stealthily insert just their bill into the school. Strangely, the sword-like object seems to go completely unnoticed by the group of fish and so does the large predator attached to it! The sailfish will then either slash their bill around or 'tap' individual prey.

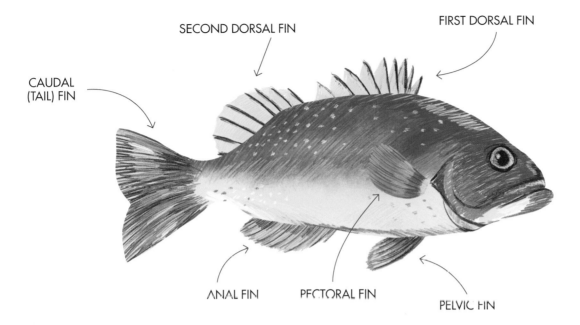

SECOND DORSAL FIN

FIRST DORSAL FIN

CAUDAL
(TAIL) FIN

ANAL FIN

PECTORAL FIN

PELVIC FIN

Because the bill is so long and the sailfish are so large and powerful, their slashing movements are extremely fast; sailfish slashing is one of the quickest **acceleration** movements of any aquatic **vertebrate**. Slashing can injure a lot of prey in one movement. The issue with this method, though, is that the injured fish still have to be caught before they can be gobbled up. Even when an animal is injured, it can still be hard to catch, and lots get away!

Tapping is a gentler approach. The sailfish use their bill to very precisely tap, disorient and isolate (but generally not injure) a single prey. They can then go straight in for the gobble. This results in a much greater chance of an immediate meal for the sailfish – they are successful in about one in three tap events. But – they only get one prey item, at most, per attempt.

Before attacks, sailfish undergo a dramatic change from their usual bluish-silver colour to almost black. This is their 'predation colouration'. They may also display stripes or even blue or orange spots over their body. Scientists are not entirely sure what the purpose of the colour change is, but it may be used as a form of communication between sailfish. These fish also extend their sail to full mast and hold their **pectoral fins** out during predation attempts. This helps them to balance and stabilise their bodies while slashing their bills around.

FAST FLYING FISH

What about air speed? You might think that's a silly question for a discussion on marine animals, but some fish can fly! And they are fast. To accommodate their unique aerial antics, flying fish have beefed-up fins, a cylindrical body and a flattened tummy. Sound familiar? It should – that is, if you've ever seen an aeroplane!

Flying fish can glide for more than 400 metres in 30 seconds. Just for comparison, the quickest human to run 400 metres took 43.03 seconds. To take off, flying fish swim towards the surface at a rate of up to 30 body lengths per second, beating their tails up to 50 times per second. It's hard even to imagine a movement that fast! These fish can reach peak air speeds in the range of 36–72 kilometres per hour. At no point do the fish actually flap their 'wings', they just glide.

Like planes, flying fish come in different shapes and sizes. Adults in the group can range from 15 centimetres to 50 centimetres. There are 'two-wingers', which rely mostly on their pectoral fins for flight, and 'four-wingers', which have enlarged pectoral and **pelvic fins**. The pelvic fins of four-wingers are used for stabilisation.

It is not entirely known why these fish fly, but the answer might be related to avoiding predators. Sometimes, one flight is not long enough to achieve whatever their goal might be. So, as their speed decreases, flying fish can just dip the lower part of their tail into the water, beat their tail back and forth (this is called taxiing), and up-up-and-away they go again.

Fins or wings? Flying fish use their fins for stabilisation, not flapping, while airborne.

Sailfish are speedy, but more importantly … stealthy!

Flappy feet

Some fish fly like birds, but some birds swim among the fish! Gentoo penguins, which are flightless, clumsy birds on land, swim elegantly. They can reach speeds of around 10 kilometres per hour.

A gentoo penguin feeds her chick.

Although they can swim relatively fast, 'porpoising', or jumping out of the water may help penguins to avoid or out-manoeuvre predators.

Sea-lebrities
ALBATROSS

Penguins may have mastered the art of swimming, but albatross have mastered the art of flying! In fact, albatross are so good at flying that they hardly ever need to flap their wings! They can ride the winds for almost as long as they want, and they typically only come to land for breeding. Albatross are true sea birds, completely reliant on the oceans for food. They are mostly found flying over the Southern Ocean and the north Pacific Ocean.

Talk about big birds! Albatross are some of the largest of all flying birds, with wingspans in some of the great albatross species (the largest of large) reaching more than 3.3 metres! These graceful gliders follow their noses to find squid, fish and crustaceans, which they catch and consume through scavenging, picking prey off from the ocean surface, or dive-bombing into the water headfirst to catch slightly deeper-swimming prey.

Albatross mostly nest in large colonies on remote islands. While raising land-bound chicks, albatross parents go on feeding trips that last around 10 days, during which time they can cover 1000 kilometres per day! That's not the only impressive flight fact on these birds though: albatross have been observed to fly around the world in just 46 days!

The Procellariiformes (pronounced: pro-sellary-a-forms), which include albatross, is one of the most threatened groups of birds. They are at risk from **introduced pests** (like rats and feral cats) that attack eggs, chicks, and nesting adults; pollution (like marine plastic debris); declining fish stocks due to humans overfishing their environments; and by **longline fishing**. Albatross and other sea birds are often attracted to the bait used on longlines; however, these baits are designed to sink quickly. Therefore, when a bird gets stuck on a hook, it gets pulled underwater and drowns.

Sometimes albatross are referred to as 'love birds'. This is because some species pair-bond, which is a scientific way of saying they mate for life. Albatross proclaim their 'love' and reconnect after long periods of separation at sea through loud, exaggerated mating dances. If one of the pair dies, the other will go through a mourning period of 1 to 2 years before beginning the quest to find a new mate.

It's easy to see how the Procellariiformes, or tubenose seabirds, get their name. The large tubes on their bill help them to get rid of the extra salt that comes along with feeding on marine animals and drinking sea water. The tubes also give them excellent smelling capabilities.

Albatross make soaring over the waves look effortless.

Salvin's albatross can dive to depths of 2 metres or more to catch a tasty treat.

NOT SO SHRIMPY

Sometimes, we talk about speed in terms of time. For example, you might have heard that something took place 'in the blink of an eye'. But if we want to be really precise, we can put a time on the action of blinking an eye: 0.27 seconds, to be exact. So, if your mum ever tells you she'll be back in the blink of an eye, you can let her know that, technically, she has already been gone too long. But if she asks, it wasn't me who taught you that!

Mantis shrimp are amazing little predatory crustaceans known for their unique speed-fuelled antics. Unlike billfish and flying fish, these shrimp do not swim at break-neck speeds or fly through the air to avoid predators. In fact, overall, they, too, move quite slowly. But despite their 'shrimpy' nature, they are not to be taken lightly.

'Smasher' mantis shrimp (which are distant relatives of the snapping shrimp discussed on pages 47–48) have a hammer-shaped **appendage** coming from their mouth region. The smash of this mouth appendage is thought to be one of the fastest movements of any living thing on the planet. In fact, it happens so fast that we can't see it without special high-speed imaging. A single strike takes just 3 milliseconds or 0.003 seconds, which means that nearly 100 strikes *could* take place in the blink of an eye. However, the shrimp are not capable of re-setting and repeating strikes that quickly.

Ironically, this super-fast movement has been designed to target creatures that are renowned for being slow – snails! Mantis shrimp love to eat snails; however, snail shells can be really tough. You would think it would take a hefty hammer (like Thor's!) to break through such a hard shell, but in the case of the mantis shrimp

Handy hammers

Smashing mantis shrimp use their hammer not only to eat but also to defend against predators, build burrows and fight with other mantis shrimp.

smash, the power comes from the hammer's speed rather than its weight or size. But how does the hammer appendage move at such speed?

Think about shooting an arrow using a bow, and now imagine trying to just throw that same arrow. Both actions rely on the muscles in your arm to fuel the movement. But, with the help of the bow, the arrow will go much further, much quicker! Mantis shrimp strikes are a lot like a bow and arrow. Instead of using its muscles to propel the appendage (like using our arm muscles to throw the arrow), mantis shrimp have anatomical machinery that works like a spring-and-latch. Setting the latch doesn't take that much energy, but when the latch is released – *BAM!* – the shrimp delivers a super punch. The power of this action is thanks to the energy being stored and then released really quickly.

Most predators who crush shell-covered prey with their jaws or claws can manipulate their prey to find just the right way of getting to the squishy prize inside. Mantis shrimp, however, need to be very precise in each hit. They know to target specific places on specific shells, since the design – and therefore the weakest point – of each type of shell is different. They also take the time to set their prey up just right before striking, by touching, probing and positioning the animal until everything is smashingly perfect. This series of manoeuvres takes, on average, a bit over 11 seconds per strike. However, there is always a chance that, even after all of this dedicated preparation, the prey might still wobble or roll out of place. Unfortunately for the shrimp, being so powerful also means that the force of their strike often rockets the prey away – they then have to start all over again! Most shells take tens, or even hundreds, of hits before the edible bit is exposed.

Eye spy

Mantis shrimp are also known for something else – they have the most complex visual system of any animal. They have a whopping 16 types of light-sensing cells (called photoreceptors), compared to the four that humans have. Even with special lenses, we still can't see everything that mantis shrimp do. Their vision is so advanced that it is impossible for us to really understand how they see their world. Why do they have such incredible eyes? It seems like they use visual signals to communicate among themselves – like a secret code that other animals can't tune in to. They can say 'I am beautiful' to a potential mate, or 'don't mess with me' to a bully, all while giving nothing at all away to potential predators. They can also move each eye separately – giving them a rather alien-like appearance!

This mantis shrimp sits outside of its burrow, just keeping an 'eye out'. Well, two eyes out, really.

Hide-and-seek

THE GAME OF LIFE

Hide-and-seek is lots of fun as a game. But, for marine animals, being able to both hide and seek is a matter of life-or-death. Animals, like the leaf scorpionfish and stonefish, are so good at hiding, in fact, that all they have to do to not be seen is stay still.

JUKKA SIITANEN

Leaf scorpionfish are experts at hiding. Can you find the fish?

You wouldn't want to step on this 'stone'! The spines on the back of stonefish transfer an extremely dangerous venom.

CAMO CRAB

One of the coolest examples of hiding in the oceans is performed by a spunky little crab. While most animals that hide through camouflage have been naturally blessed with perfect colouration or patterning, this ability doesn't always come wrapped in a birthday suit. Decorator crabs have an unusual form of anti-**carnivore** camouflage: they have developed a way to physically become a part of their surroundings!

Decorator crabs put a lot of effort into blending in. First, they search for the perfect material, such as sponge, algae, anemone, or a variety of other biological beauties. Then, they clip a chunk off and chew it up! They don't do this to test the taste; instead, their chewing helps to soften the ends of their new attire. They then rub the chewed-up material back and forth over their shell until it sticks just right. Their shells are covered in special Velcro-like hairs for this exact purpose – to lock-on decorations. These stiff hairs can be hooked, bent or straight, and they allow the crabs to attach a variety of different decorations. The straight hairs have even smaller hairs on them that feed information back to the crab on how their decorations are holding up!

By the time they're fully 'dressed', decorator crabs don't look like crabs at all. They don't even have crab-shaped outlines anymore. However, to be convincing in their disguise of 'reef' or 'rock', these crabs need to spend most of their time motionless. Otherwise, a walking chunk of reef would surely attract attention!

ED BIERMAN

Would you recognise this as a crab? If you look really closely, you can just make out the legs!

Sea-lebrities
CHRISTMAS TREE WORM

DENICE ASKEBRINK

Not a tree, and not even a plant, these Christmas tree look-alikes are … worms!

Christmas tree worms are colourful, bristly, tube-building, segmented worms. They are a species of annelid, just like earthworms and leeches. These 3–4-centimetre **sedentary** worms are found throughout the world's tropical oceans. Christmas tree worms ooze a chalky calcium carbonate tube around their otherwise soft bodies – and this becomes their home. They often build their tubes on coral, which continues to grow around them and further cements them in.

When they are safe from predators, these worms stick two Christmas-tree-shaped crowns out of the top of the tube. The rest of the body stays hidden. The 'trees' are actually spirals of small tentacles with lots of little hair-like structures on them. The worms use these to breathe and trap micro-prey (like **phytoplankton**) that floats by.

At the first hint of a predator, the worms quickly hide themselves in their tubes. They even use their operculum, which is the animal version of a front door, to plug the tube's entrance. You might have seen a startled snail in your yard do the same thing. Christmas tree worm opercula are covered in sharp, branched spines, though!

These bright little worms have a big job: they help to protect their coral hosts. Interestingly, coral adorned with Christmas tree worms recovers from damage – such as bleaching, predation and nasty algal growth – quicker than coral without worms!

In case these disguise strategies weren't impressive enough already, some decorator crabs take their wondrous wardrobes even further. They carefully and selectively choose decorations that come with their own defences (like anemones with stinging capability, or algae that is poisonous or just plain yuck when eaten). It makes sense – if the goal is *not* to be eaten, then there is no point covering yourself with something even more delicious than you are! Ultimately, not only do these clever crabs not look like crabs, but they wouldn't smell or taste like crabs either. Genius!

LOOKING UP

Flatfish, an order that includes turbot, soles, flounders and halibut, are another extreme example of what animals go through to hide. Hide, that is, right out on the ocean floor!

For the first few days of their life, summer flounder are familiarly fish-shaped fish. They are upright, **symmetrical** and just plain ordinary. But then, after a week or two, something fishy starts to happen – the flounder start to swim with a tilt. It's like all of a sudden, they lose the concept of 'up' (which is normally determined by where the light comes from and gravity) and they start to lean to one side. At first, their lean is hardly noticeable. But then they get tilty-er, and tilty-er. By the time they are around a month old, they swim completely on their side.

Then, as if this were not strange enough already, they begin to go through a major remodelling process. For a start, *their eyes move across their head*! The 'down' eye – the one that was facing the bottom of the ocean after 'the big tilt' – moves to the top of the head. The 'up' eye doesn't stay put, either: it shifts over to make more space. These fish live out their lives with two wonky, upwards facing eyes (that can creepily move independently of each other), a sideways mouth and a seriously blind underside! They spend less and less time swimming, and more and more time on the bottom. From this position, their crazy but efficient eyes allow them to see in every direction!

To go through such a major change, a lot needs to happen to these extraordinary, **asymmetrical** fish. Some of their bones thin down and even deform to allow for the eye movements. The fish's fins also change to better allow for their new sideways method of swimming. The bits of their brain that take note of pesky little things like gravity also adjust to make everything seem right again!

FROM FISH TO FLATFISH

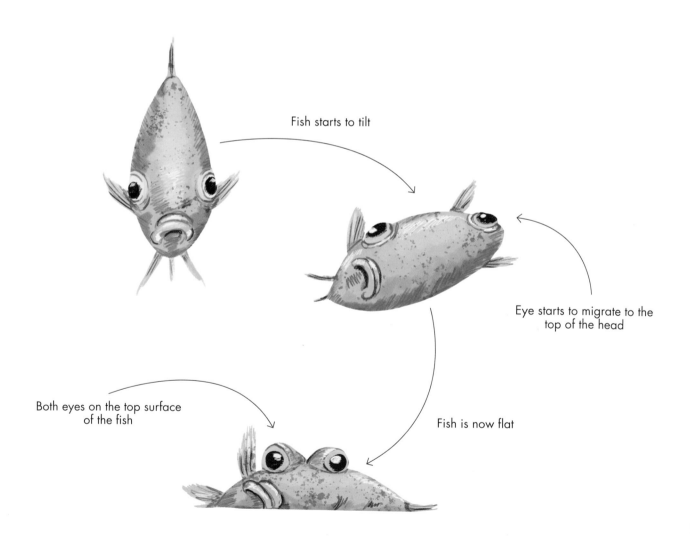

Fish starts to tilt

Eye starts to migrate to the top of the head

Both eyes on the top surface of the fish

Fish is now flat

DENICE ASKEBRINK

Flatfish always keep their eyes to the sky.

Flatfish are ideally suited to just lying about motionless on the bottom. Their body colouration and patterns blend in well with sandy **substrate**, but they can also change their colours to match different environments. Some of these fish can change colour in as little as 2–8 seconds! They can also bury themselves in the substrate for extra hiding power. Having both eyes on the top of their head helps with this – they can, quite literally, keep their eyes out, even when the rest of their body is buried!

Righty or lefty?

Some humans are right-handed, and some are left-handed. Similarly, some flatfish have both eyes on their left side, whereas others have both eyes on their right side. Different species of flatfish show different side preferences; most individuals within a species will tilt the same way, but not all!

Crocodile fish have the most incredible eyes, but they're designed not to be seen!

HIDDEN GEMS

Crocodile fish are members of the flathead **family** (yes, they have flat heads!). Like the flatfish, these flat-fronted animals have detailed body colouration that allows them to blend in with sand and rubble. And, also like the flatfish, their eyes stick up on the top of their heads. Unfortunately, although providing lots of visual benefits, few things scream '*I'm here, EAT ME*' more than big, bulging eyes! So, to help keep themselves off the marine menu, crocodile fish have developed something called 'iris lappets'. The iris is the coloured part of the eye – for example, you might have blue, brown or green irises – and iris lappets are little branched bits of flesh that partially cover the iris. In the crocodile fish, the iris lappets are coloured to look just like grains of sand! Camouflage complete!

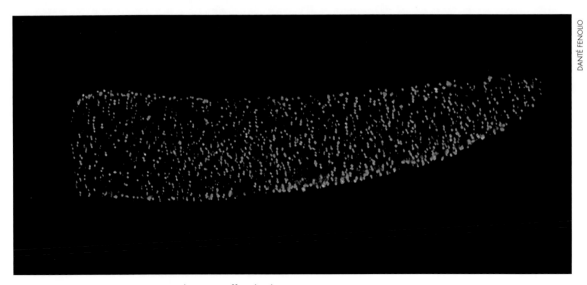

DANTÉ FENOLIO

A deep-sea pyrosome (tunicate) showing off its bioluminescence.

BLINDED BY THE LIGHT

Bioluminescence (discussed in Chapter 4) is a key tool for both hiding and seeking activities in dimly lit ocean environments. That's right – not only can light help animals to seek out prey, but amazingly, it can also help animals to hide from predators. 'Twilight' zones of the ocean are where it is not quite light and not quite dark. Only a small amount of light from the sun, moon or stars filters through to these watery depths, creating a dim environment. In these zones, animals are **silhouetted** against the light from the surface when viewed from below. This makes it very difficult for animals that swim off the bottom to hide! As a result, some fish, krill, squid and even sharks have learned to use bioluminescence to light up their bellies, helping them to blend into the light! Certain species are so good at this that they can even match the amount of light that filters through the water. If a cloud passes overhead, no problem: they just hit the dimmer on their belly lights!

Twilight treasures

We currently know so little about animals of the twilight zone that when scientists embark on voyages to explore these realms, they may discover new species at a rate of almost 7 per hour!

READY OR NOT, HERE I COME …

With all the great marine hiders, there is no surprise that there are also some expert seekers. Marine animals use a range of senses to understand their vast, three-dimensional, watery environment. Some of these, like vision, hearing and smell, are familiar to us, while others, like **electroreception** and **echolocation**, are not.

THE BETTER TO SEEK YOU WITH

Sharks and their close relatives have gained an advantage in the big marine game of hide-and-seek. They have a 'sixth sense' called electroreception. Electroreception allows them to sense the electrical activity of other animals – for example, a beating heart. Some sharks are so good at picking up on electrical activity, that they can seek out buried animals, even when they lie completely motionless!

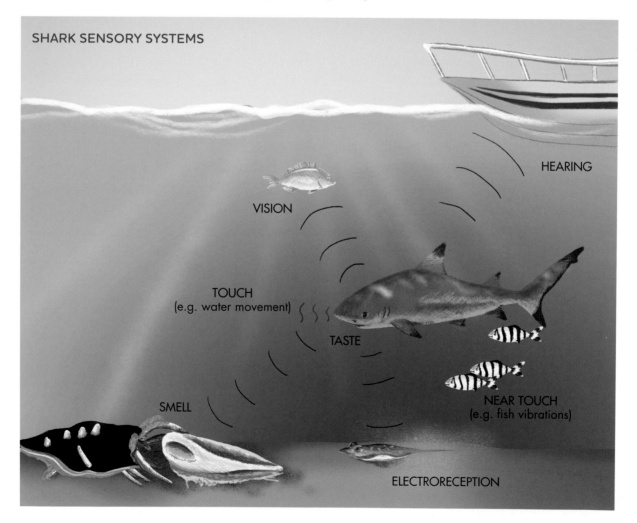

SHARK SENSORY SYSTEMS

HEARING

VISION

TOUCH
(e.g. water movement)

TASTE

NEAR TOUCH
(e.g. fish vibrations)

SMELL

ELECTRORECEPTION

Don't ... move ... a muscle

Electrical activity in the marine world can be a dead giveaway, even from the best hiding spots. In the final stage before birth, sharks that develop in egg cases will hold their breath, wrap their tails around their bodies and keep super-still when they sense danger. This demonstrates that they can use their sensory systems to detect the presence of predators – and that they already know to be worried about them! It also shows that they are brainy enough to figure out ways to protect themselves even while stuck in an egg. All this ... before they are even born!

BLAKE CHAPMAN

Around two-thirds of baby sharks develop internally (inside the mother) and are born live, whereas the other third develop externally (in the water) protected by tough egg cases. By clearing away some of the sticky, stringy outer layers of the egg case and holding it in front of a light, you can see the developing baby shark inside. This one has its head to the left and its flexible (already stripey) tail wrapped around the nutritious yolk that gives it the energy it needs to grow. In this image, you can see one of the still largely see-through pectoral fins at the top-right. The shark's developing eyes are only just visible.

ECHOLOCATION

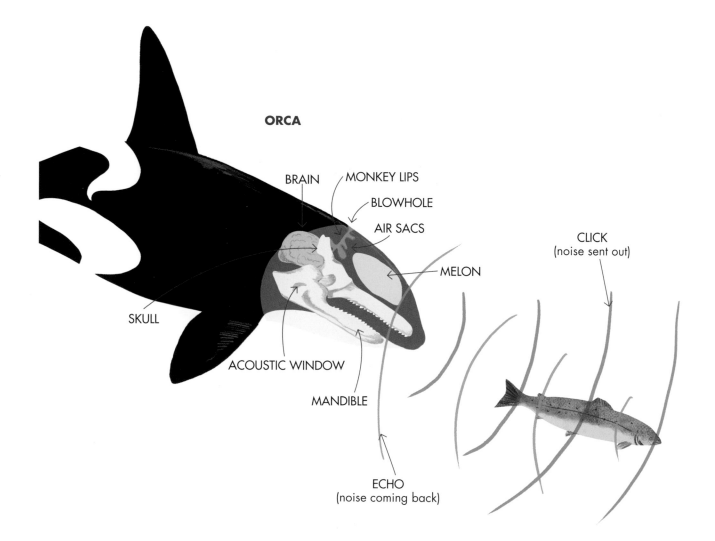

ORCA

BRAIN

MONKEY LIPS

BLOWHOLE

AIR SACS

MELON

SKULL

ACOUSTIC WINDOW

MANDIBLE

CLICK
(noise sent out)

ECHO
(noise coming back)

Orca whales, on the other hand, utilise an entirely different strategy: they rely heavily on echolocation for seeking out their prey. Echo-(echo)-lo-(lo)-cation-(cation-cation-cation) relies on decoding the echoes of emitted sounds. We can do this, too – at least to an extent. If you go into an empty room and yell out, you'll often hear the noise repeating – these are echoes. The larger the room, the longer it will take for the echoes to come back. However, that's about the extent of the information we are able to gain from echoes. **Cetaceans** do it much better!

Toothed whales and dolphins, like orcas, pilot whales and bottlenose dolphins, use echolocation for hunting and navigating. They can produce a variety of sounds by moving air between pockets in their head. Many marine echolocators even have bulging foreheads due to the advantage of having a large fatty pocket in their head that helps to produce 'clicks'. Funnily enough, this anatomical feature is called the melon! Sound reflections are picked up by a specialised part of the animal's lower jaw, before being passed to the middle ear for processing.

Sound travels through water much more easily than it does in air. And, as a bonus (as compared to our visual capability, at least), sound travels in all directions. Therefore, echoes can quickly paint a detailed picture of the surroundings. Orcas can tell from echoes how large or small and how near or far objects are. They can detect the sea floor, the shore, underwater obstacles, water depth, and other animals that may be nearby. Orcas are so sensitive to sound that they can tell the difference between closely related salmon species through echoes alone!

Sing-song

The whistles, clicks, groans and other noises made by toothed whales are thought to be important in communication between individuals as well as for feeding. In contrast, baleen whales, such as humpbacks and fin whales, produce a series of sounds that are often termed 'songs'. These are used just for communicating. This makes sense, seeing as their favourite food, plankton, wouldn't require such a 'resounding' search strategy.

AILIE SUZUKI

A small pod of orcas travels together close to the coast.

Go with the flow

CURRENT UNDERSTANDING

Although we talk about five different oceans (Pacific, Atlantic, Indian, Arctic and Southern), plus a variety of seas, these are actually just the pieces of one great big, salty body of water. There are no physical barriers or borders between the oceans. But this doesn't mean that all oceans are the same. Although ocean conditions differ in different parts of the world, the currents ensure these bodies of water stay connected. Currents move (and sometimes even prevent the movement of) water, heat, nutrients, and some animals and plants – all around the globe. A drop of water that wets your toes at the beach washes away to go somewhere else. And then it goes somewhere else again. In fact, it travels all around the globe until it makes it right back to where it started from (or at least close by). But it won't tickle your toes again – its round trip will take around a thousand years!

Current issues

Ocean currents are important to more than just the oceans. Heat from warm surface water is absorbed by the atmosphere, warming the air as well. If currents slow down, more heat is released. This makes our climate warmer.

OCEAN CURRENTS

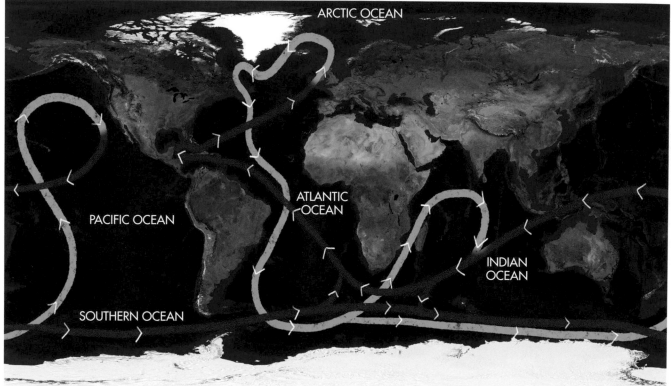

BEST-BACKGROUNDS/SHUTTERSTOCK/ASTRED HICKS

GREY NURSE SHARKS

DENICE ASKEBRINK

Grey nurse sharks are often mistaken for white sharks. However, they are very different animals. The unfortunate reality for grey nurse sharks is that they do look quite scary. They are large (reaching 3-plus metres in length), bulky, browny-grey sharks, with round bodies and pointy snouts. They are often seen 'hovering' in water currents or swimming around sluggishly. Depending on how strong the current is, they will either slowly open and close their mouths to pull oxygenated water over their gills, or just face into the current and let the water movement do all the work for them. Staying still saves valuable energy compared to their relatives that need to keep moving to keep breathing. But, because of their passive ways, passers-by are almost always given a detailed view of their rows of large, pointy teeth.

These sharks are not always sluggish, though, and are capable of lightning-fast attacks on prey. They can extend their jaws out and away from their skull in a swift movement that gives them extra reach, extra speed and a greater gape (which is, non-technically, the 'ahhhhh-factor'). They can also 'crack' their powerful tail, which provides their large bodies with a burst of speed. Underwater, these tail cracks sound like the crack of a whip!

While grey nurse sharks are generally considered to be docile and have an almost complete disregard for humans, unfortunately, the opposite can't be said. Because of their toothy appearance, many people thought they were better dead than alive; those people nearly succeeded in wiping out entire grey nurse shark populations.

They may look scary with their rows of long, pointy, inward-facing teeth, but grey nurse sharks have far more to fear from us, than we do from them!

Grey nurse sharks became the first species of shark to be protected anywhere in the world. This happened in 1984 in New South Wales, Australia. These sharks are still protected today across most of their Australian range. Despite being protected, grey nurse sharks are sometimes fished illegally, and they are caught accidentally by commercial and recreational fishers as well as by shark control programs. The eastern Australian population is classified as 'critically endangered' and, sadly, is still decreasing.

They do what??

Grey nurse sharks have some really unique characteristics. For one, they uniquely (among sharks) gulp air from the surface and store it in their stomachs to assist with buoyancy! They also exhibit a behaviour called 'intrauterine cannibalism'. In simpler terms, this means that early in development and long before birth, the oldest **embryo** will develop an 'egg tooth' and eat the other embryos and eggs around it. This allows the baby to grow really big over its 9–12-month development; it will be around 1 metre in length when it's born. Ironically, once they are born, they grow quite slowly.

The closer water gets to the freezing cold north and south poles, the cooler it gets. In the extremely cold Arctic and Antarctic, some of that water even freezes into ice. When oceanic water freezes, the salt is left behind, making the surrounding water even saltier. When water becomes saltier, it also becomes denser – or thicker – and it sinks. Lighter, less salty water moves in to take its place. That simple action is responsible for driving global ocean currents! The Antarctic Circumpolar Current (ACC) in the Southern Ocean, for example, moves 145 million cubic metres of water *every second*! No wonder it is known as the 'mightiest current in the oceans'. Remarkably, the ACC carries more than 100 times the flow of all the rivers on Earth!

Sea-lebrities
TUNICATES

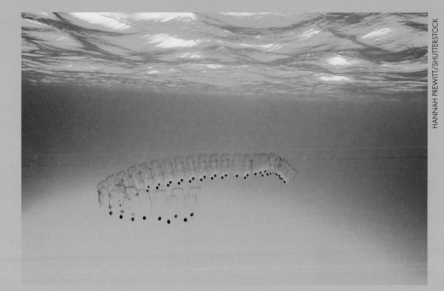

HANNAH PREWITT/SHUTTERSTOCK

Salps, and other tunicates, are nature's water pistols.

Tunicates, or sea squirts, as they are commonly called, are marine invertebrates. Tunicates are an awesome rock pool find! When touched or startled, these natural little pistols shoot water! After their planktonic **larval** stage, most tunicates stick fast to a surface of some variety – like coral, rocks, docks, or even the shells of fellow invertebrates.

Other tunicates float through the water for their entire lives. Salps, for example, look like floating plastic bags with a little bit of stuff left in them. They are short, 10-centimetre sac-like tubes that are completely transparent, except for their gut (which often appears red from eating red algae). Salps eat by sucking water in, filtering and digesting the algae, then squirting the leftover water out. This squirting is also what propels them.

Salps float around on their own for a while, but then link up with other salps to form chains that can be more than 4 metres in length. They continue through life this way: floating, filtering, eating and squirting as a team (search 'sea salp chain' online to see what I mean!). Interestingly, engineers have studied how salps swarm together and form 'salp chains' when searching for food. This animal insight has helped them to solve a variety of challenging problems!

Antarctic pelagic salps sometimes form extensive, dense blooms (or large aggregations). These blooms are most extreme in warmer years, when there is less sea ice. The problem with salps is that they compete with krill for food. Lots of things in the Antarctic food web eat krill, but few things eat salps, so this can throw off the natural balance at the very base of the food chain. Repeated and increasingly warm years could seriously threaten krill populations, consequently also endangering the food supply of larger plankton-loving animals like whales.

THE UPSIDE

In the surface waters of the ocean, heat and light energy from the sun fuel the growth of marine plants and algae. These are rich sources of food for other animals in the food chain and attract lots of hungry mouths. But with all of the growing and eating, surface water can quickly become depleted of nutrients. At the same time, sources of nutrients that don't float – like bits of dead animals – sink down to deep waters and the ocean floor. While the surface waters become low in nutrients, the deeper waters become higher in nutrients. This is a tough break for animals that stay close to the ocean's surface!

Here's where upwelling currents come in to save the day! Upwelling currents are caused by winds that blow across the surface of the ocean. These winds push nutrient-depleted surface water aside, and cool, nutrient-rich water rises up to take its place – putting all those nutrients right where they are needed the most. The areas with the strongest upwelling currents, like around Antarctica, are where you'll often find some of the most voracious consumers – such as baleen whales. Many other animals also take advantage of these highly productive areas!

AILIE SUZUKI

The upwelling of nutrient-rich surface water is critical for the survival of extra-large blue whales, and (relatively) tiny puffins.

WITH UPS THERE ARE DOWNS

Downwelling currents are equally as important as upwelling currents. Downwelling occurs when water is pushed together and forced down. This happens when currents converge or when wind pushes surface water against physical barriers, like land. While deep water brings much-needed nutrients to the surface, surface water has all-important oxygen. Oxygen becomes dissolved in the ocean when air mixes with surface water. Oxygen is also produced in the oceans by organisms that use **photosynthesis** to make energy, like plants and algae. These plants are always near the surface, though, since they can only grow in reach of sunlight.

UPWELLING AND DOWNWELLING CURRENTS

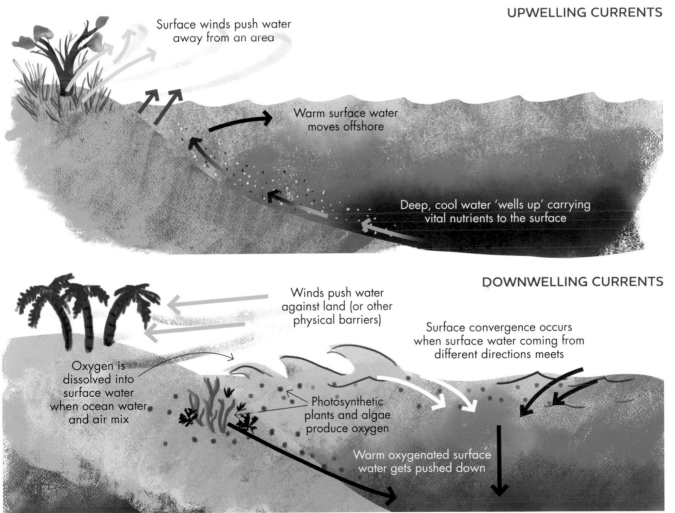

UPWELLING CURRENTS

Surface winds push water away from an area

Warm surface water moves offshore

Deep, cool water 'wells up' carrying vital nutrients to the surface

DOWNWELLING CURRENTS

Winds push water against land (or other physical barriers)

Surface convergence occurs when surface water coming from different directions meets

Oxygen is dissolved into surface water when ocean water and air mix

Photosynthetic plants and algae produce oxygen

Warm oxygenated surface water gets pushed down

Like nutrients on the surface, oxygen can be consumed quickly in the deep sea. Without the transfer of oxygen from surface waters down to the deep, almost all deep-sea life would cease to exist. Some scientists believe this could happen if oceans continue to get warmer. Warm water carries less oxygen than cooler water, so warmer downwelling currents transport less oxygen to deep-sea environments. Animals also breathe faster in warm water, using up the oxygen that is available more quickly.

DENICE ASKEBRINK

Even the biggest predatory fish in the sea, the white shark, relies on ocean currents for delivering the good stuff.

NOAA OKEANOS EXPLORER PROGRAM, 2013
NORTHEAST U.S. CANYONS EXPEDITION

Downwelling currents are so important for deep-sea animals, like this amazing Rhinochimaera.

JUST DRIFTIN'

When we think about the most important marine animals, our minds don't generally rush to plankton. But they should! Plankton form the base of the oceanic food chain. Whales, sharks, dolphins, fish and even coral reefs are entirely reliant on these little floaties. It is a good thing that, with the exception of bacteria, plankton are the most abundant organisms on Earth! And these fantastic floaties are completely reliant on the currents.

Plankton is the generic name for organisms that cannot swim against the current. They are made up of countless different species and can be either plants (phytoplankton) or animals (**zooplankton**). Plankton are usually tiny, but can be larger. In fact, plankton are so amazingly diverse that in a single gulp a whale shark could swallow 15 or more **phyla** of animals. You can learn more about marine animal phyla on page 136.

DRIFTING FOR FOOD

Many marine species have a planktonic period. This is usually when they are in eggs or while they are still small or not fully developed. These animals float along as plankton until they are able to sink (permanently) or swim. Even some of the biggest and strongest marine animals, like tuna, drift their early days away as plankton.

The western rock lobster, which is an important fisheries species found off Western Australia, is a spiny crustacean that has a 9- to 11-month larval period. With the aid of winds, the early-stage **larvae**, called phyllosoma, drift as far as 1500 kilometres offshore to open ocean habitats. During this time, they go through a series of moults that take them from 2 millimetres long at hatching to around 35 millimetres long in the final larval stage. These offshore movements are crucial, as they expose the growing larvae to key food resources – like phytoplankton – that they need to mature into healthy adults.

Western rock lobster larvae rely on currents to transport them offshore, where there is more of the food that they need to grow big and strong.

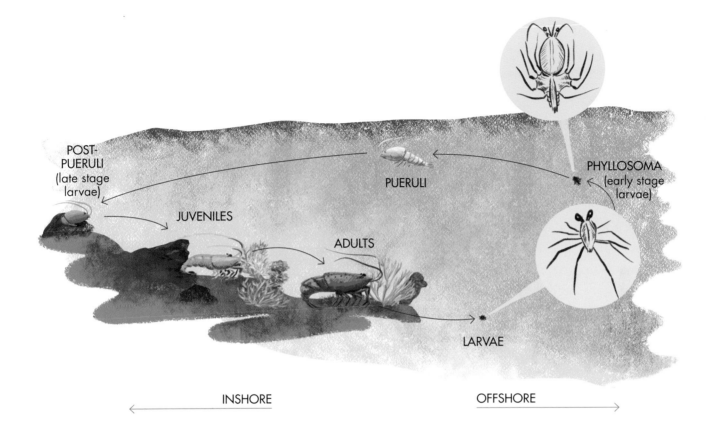

POST-
PUERULI
(late stage
larvae)

JUVENILES

PUERULI

ADULTS

PHYLLOSOMA
(early stage
larvae)

LARVAE

INSHORE

OFFSHORE

Most western rock lobster larvae don't survive long enough to reach late larval stages. However, those that do survive will go through another moult that totally changes their appearance and transforms them into perfect, but transparent, miniature (25 millimetres long) lobsters. They are known as pueruli, and it is at this point that they are ready to start their journey back towards the near-shore environments they will call home as adults. Their return to those habitats is aided by the strong eastward movements of the Leeuwin Current. Amazingly, the little lobsters don't eat at all during this journey – relying instead on energy reserves they developed while offshore. The lobsters will only survive if the winds and currents carry them back to just the right environment. Well, that … and if they aren't eaten on the way!

PLANKTON FOR LIFE

Many planktonic organisms leave the drifting community as they mature. However, others, like some copepods, stay as plankton their whole life. Copepod comes from the Greek words meaning 'paddle feet'. Copepods are capable of short bursts of movement – either to escape predators or to ambush prey. They are arguably the most important of all zooplankton, and they may be the most abundant group of animals on Earth.

Copepods have two extremely important jobs: (1) to eat, and (2) to produce more copepods. While a life of eating may sound easy, or even dream-like for us, it is not something to be taken lightly for copepods. They need to filter huge volumes of water through their body every day to survive long enough to complete job number two. And when I say huge, I mean *huge*. Like, 10 000 000-times-their-own-body-volume huge!

I guess, technically, copepods have three jobs. Their third job is to *be* eaten. Copepods are so important to the base of the marine food chain that you could go so far as to say that the weight of the (marine) world rests on their little paddle feet.

It's amazing to think that even these large, spiny lobsters start out as plankton.

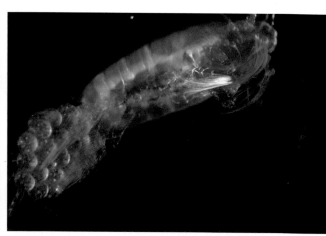

Although teeny-tiny, the marine world relies on planktonic organisms, like this copepod!

Dirty drifters

Sadly, another thing that goes with the flow is plastic. When plastic ends up in the oceans, it is bad news! Around 60% of the plastics we produce float and are carried by winds and currents. Unfortunately, just because they get transported out of sight, it does not mean that they have gone away. In some places around the world, major rubbish accumulation zones – or garbage patches – have developed. The Great Pacific Garbage Patch located in subtropical waters off the western United States is estimated to have at least 79 000 tonnes of plastic floating over an area of 1 600 000 square kilometres. By weight, more than half of this is discarded or lost fishing nets. However, tiny pieces of plastic (less than 5 millimetres in size), or microplastics, make up 94% of the approximately *1 800 000 000 000 pieces* of floating rubbish. Although mini, microplastics are a MEGA problem! Marine animals are mistaking plastic for food, or helplessly ingesting it while filter feeding. But, ingesting too much plastic can kill even the largest of marine animals. To help prevent the situation from getting worse, everyone needs to play their part: please, skip the straw, bail on buying balloons and just say 'no!' to single-use plastic in general!

Plastic is a big problem in our oceans. How many individual pieces of plastic can you count in this small area of beach?

POLAR BRRRRRRRRRS

Being on opposite sides of the planet is not the only difference between the Arctic and Antarctic. In fact, they truly are polar opposites! Currents are one reason behind some of these differences. Antarctica is (generally) ice-covered land surrounded by ocean. The Arctic, on the other hand, is ocean that is almost entirely surrounded by land. The land around the Arctic forms a barrier to water flow and, more notably, the movement of sea ice. With little other place to go, Arctic ice floes – which are just large chunks of floating ice – bump into each other and pile up. This makes Arctic ice thicker than Antarctic ice, which moves around with far fewer barriers.

Being thicker – usually around 2–3 metres deep – about half of the Arctic ice lasts through the summer. In contrast, less than 20% of the 1–2-metre-thick Antarctic ice survives the summer. Nevertheless, this usually still leaves around 3 million square kilometres of ice.

The animals of these two regions also couldn't be more different. No terrestrial mammals live in the Antarctic, whereas the Arctic supports a variety of these

Although polar bears spend a large part of their time on land, they are completely reliant on marine ecosystems.

animals. This includes the extraordinary polar bears. Polar bears live mostly on land and sea ice, but they are considered marine mammals because they are heavily dependent on the marine environment for their food, which includes seals and whales.

Despite their fluffy appearance, polar bears are excellent swimmers. They have large front paws that are slightly webbed and act like paddles. It's mind-boggling to think of needing to cool down in the Arctic, but this is one reason polar bears go swimming! When hunting, they can swim for hundreds of kilometres over days; however, swimming is more tiring and uses far more energy than walking. It also takes a lot of energy just to keep a wet bear warm in these icy waters. Really long swims, which are required when sea ice is scarce, can have serious consequences to the bears' health. Sadly, they are sometimes even fatal. Polar bear cubs are not as good at swimming, and they also have far less fat than adults. Therefore, they get cold much more easily, making them especially reliant on the sanctuary provided by sea ice.

Polar bears are excellent swimmers.

When the Arctic sea ice is thick and strong enough to support the predatory movements of the bears, they hunt and feed. However, when the ice breaks apart and gets carried away in the currents, their marine prey becomes inaccessible, and the bears are forced to move to land. During this time, they have to survive on their built-up fat reserves. As the icy season becomes shorter and shorter due to our global temperature becoming warmer and warmer, polar bears have less time to eat and have to survive for longer without food. The loss of sea ice due to climate change is the most important threat to these animals. Scientists are concerned that polar bear populations could decline by a tragic 30% in just 35 years.

Sea ice is super cool – and super important. But sadly, it's not staying cool enough to support some marine mammals, like polar bears.

Water bears vs water bears

While polar bears are bears that rely on water, water bears, or tardigrades, are teeny-tiny, plump, eight-legged, segmented aquatic animals. Upon microscopic examination, tardigrades look like chubby little millimetre-or-so-long bears that clumsily crawl around. Tardigrades are found pretty much anywhere where there is water. And by anywhere, I mean anywhere! They are found from the Arctic to the Antarctic, in salt water, fresh water, thermal hot springs, under ice sheets, and even on dry land that only *sometimes* gets wet. They are found from the dark abyssal depths of the seas to the top of the Himalayan Mountains! These little guys can dry out almost entirely and withstand some of the most extreme conditions imaginable, including long-term starvation, temperatures from -273°C to nearly 100°C, a complete lack of oxygen, exceedingly high pressure (to 7.5 gigapascals), exposure to high doses of irradiation and even direct exposure to outer space! So cool!

3DSTOCK/SHUTTERSTOCK

In contrast to polar bears, teeny-tiny water bears, or tardigrades, thrive in a wide variety of environments!

Chapter 8

Deadly animals

Some animals are known above all else for one thing: being deadly! These animals are certainly worth knowing about – in particular, the potentially dangerous animals that live in the places we like to visit. One such example is the blue-ringed octopus.

Although we might think of some animals as deadly, dangerous, or even scary, these animals are not out to get us. Instead, they are just doing what they need to do – which is eating, defending themselves and trying to survive in their big, bad watery world! Going to the beach and playing in the surf can be tonnes of fun and a great experience, but we do need to remember that these are wild and uncontrollable places. There are lots of things to be mindful of when visiting marine environments – the animals that live there are just one of those things. But learning more about potentially dangerous animals makes it easier to respect and appreciate them, rather than fear them.

THE POINTY END

If I asked you to think of the most dangerous, most scary, most *DEADLY* animal in the ocean, what would you picture? My guess is that it would not be a box jellyfish, Irukandji jellyfish, blue-ringed octopus or lionfish. I'd even be willing to go further and bet that your image isn't one of a sea snake, cone snail or stingray – although all of these can be deadly! Instead, I bet that your mind has gone straight to … sharks! And all for good reason – sharks are indeed super deadly … to other marine animals. Sharks are also super amazing!

There are well over 500 different species of sharks, and there is an enormous amount of diversity within the group. There are huge sharks and small sharks, fat sharks and flat sharks. There are big sharks that eat little things and little sharks that eat big things. And, of course, big sharks that eat big things. In summary, there is no 'typical' shark. But each is a deadly predator to *something*! The sharks that we consider to be most deadly, though, include white sharks, tiger sharks and bull sharks – because they can kill big things. These sharks are large, muscular and have extremely powerful jaws. And, they have rows and rows of killer teeth.

Hammerheads might not have nails, but they do have teeth!

Sea-lebrities
BLUE-RINGED OCTOPUS

SIMON J PIERCE

A blue-ringed octopus can look so small and squishy, but don't be tempted to poke it – their venom can be deadly.

Blue-ringed octopuses are both spectacular and spectacularly venomous little animals. Normally, these animals are quite dull, blending into their drab sandy and rocky environments, which include coastal rock pools. But, if disturbed or threatened, they flash around 60 bright blue rings across their tiny 10-centimetre bodies. These octopuses have excellent control over their colouration, and their blue rings can be 'turned on' or 'turned off' very quickly.

Why blue? Blue-ringed octopuses are actually quite peaceful little animals that simply want to be left alone. Just because they have killer venom, doesn't mean they want to use it! So, they broadcast their 'please don't make me hurt you' message in blue, since blue is the colour that many shallow-water predators, like fish, marine mammals and birds, see best!

While their colouration is cool, it serves as a warning only. It is their bite that really packs a venomous punch. In fact, these octopuses use the same neurotoxin, TTX, that pufferfish use (see Chapter 2). Blue-ringed octopus venom is so strong and fast-acting that, if not quickly and properly attended to, it can kill a human. It is a nasty venom, too, which causes paralysis. Death typically results from a lack of oxygen. Yet, the paralysis only targets certain muscles, so the animal bitten remains awake and alert, despite not being able to move. Yikes! If you are lucky enough to see a blue-ringed octopus while exploring a rock pool, just enjoy viewing it from afar!

ROW, ROW, ROW

Most species of sharks have 20–30 rows of teeth; however, whale sharks can have up to 300! Whereas we only get two shots at teeth – our baby teeth and adult teeth – sharks continuously lose and grow new teeth throughout their lives. When one of their teeth becomes blunt, broken, lost, or just old, it gets replaced with a brand-new, sharp, shiny one. Sharks can go through thousands or even tens of thousands of teeth in their lifetime! The rate that sharks' teeth are replaced varies, depending on the species, the animal's age, diet, water temperature and even the season! For example, each 'front' tooth in a nurse shark is replaced as quickly as every 8–10 days in the summer, but only every 70 days in the winter.

When talking about sharks' teeth, 'rows' go from the front of the jaw to the back. That is, a row is made up of the functional tooth at the front of the mouth, and the replacement teeth that are found behind it. The line of functional teeth that run along the front of the jaw (including one tooth from each row), like what we have in our mouths, is called a 'series'.

CLINT CHAPMAN

Sharks are so reliant on having effective teeth that they make sure they always have lots of spares on-hand – or, more appropriately, in-jaw!

Tooth-tastic!

The now-extinct megalodon shark had teeth as large as 18 centimetres long! This means that a single one of their teeth would have been roughly the size of your head!

Different sharks eat different things and have different methods of hunting, so it makes sense that they also have different teeth. Goblin shark teeth are long and spikey and designed for catching fish and squid. This is perfect, since squid are a preferred prey of goblin sharks. However, they would be pretty useless at crushing through sea urchins – a favourite food of Port Jackson sharks. Luckily, Port Jackson shark teeth are small, and made of a combination of some sharp and some blunt crushing teeth. Although cookiecutter sharks and white sharks both feed on seals, cookiecutter shark teeth are small and triangular and designed for surgically removing a plug of flesh. Their teeth would be painfully inefficient at ripping and tearing through an entire seal – which is what white sharks need to be able to do! Just like us, most sharks have a variety of sizes and shapes of teeth in their jaws. This allows them to do all the different things they need to do to catch and eat their prey, like bite, tear, spear, rip, crush, saw, and even latch on.

BE SHARK SMART

Although we tend to think of sharks as being scary and deadly, it's only other aquatic animals that really need to be fearful of them. However, sharks are powerful, curious and protective, and they deserve complete respect. If we enter their environment, then we do face a risk of being injured by them – or worse. However, the chances of this happening are *extremely* low. Only around 5–10 people around the whole world are killed by sharks every year. This number is much smaller than for many other animals that humans interact with. These include all of the obvious suspects, like lions, hippos and crocodiles, but also some that may surprise you, like cows, horses and pet dogs!

Predator or prey?

Surprisingly, nearly every species of shark has natural predators. In many cases, these are other sharks. Even adult white sharks can be killed by orca whales, meaning that in these ecosystems, the sharks are not the **apex predator**!

AILIE SUZUKI

Playing with your food takes on a whole new meaning when you're an orca! These mighty marine mammals seem to be enjoying passing around a thresher shark they caught.

If you are scared of sharks, then going for a swim in the ocean can be intimidating. Luckily, there are some things you can do to help keep yourself safe. The most important thing is to always swim at patrolled beaches. This will help to make sure you are safe from all of the risks the oceans can pose, not just sharks. It's also a really good idea to always swim with other people, in clear water and when there is lots of light.

To see sharks up close, you can visit them at an aquarium. Then you'll soon see that they are not the scary eating machines they are often made out to be! This can be an especially important step if you are really terrified of sharks.

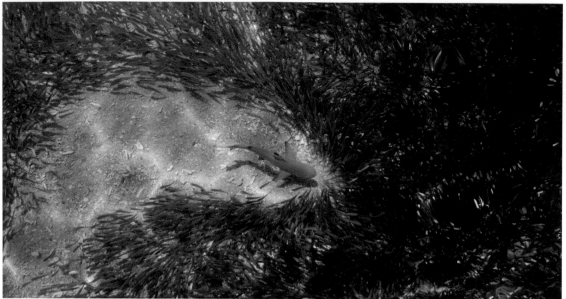

KRIS MIKAEL KRISTER ON UNSPLASH

Schooling fish present excellent feeding opportunities for sharks – as well as many other marine predators – so if you see 'bait balls' like this in the water, it's best to watch the action from the safety of dry land.

Ultimately, the one thing we should never do is try to remove sharks of any species from the oceans for our own benefit or safety. After all, the marine environment is their world, and sharks – as well as many of the other potentially deadly marine animals – are absolutely essential to the health of their ecosystems and the oceans overall!

DENICE ASKEBRINK

Tiger sharks are stunning, but also extremely powerful and adept predators.

WHITE-SPOTTED EAGLE RAY

White-spotted eagle rays are known for launching themselves into the air.

CLINT CHAPMAN

Although they are more notably known for their striking beauty, white-spotted eagle rays can inflict serious wounds with the venomous barbs on their tail. These distinctive rays have broad, pointy wings that can have a span of 2 metres; a v-shaped snout; a long, long tail; and white spots all over their dark disc (or body). But their tummies are white. White-spotted eagle rays are most often found in small groups, swimming near the surface in the open water of tropical and subtropical oceans. Sometimes, they leap clear out of the water. In extremely random events, they have even leapt into boats!

Stingrays have strong, whip-like tails that can be lashed around quickly. However, people are most often injured by these animals when they accidentally step on rays that are lying on the sand or when trying to unhook them from fishing gear.

While all stingrays are rays, not all rays are stingrays! In fact, of the over 600 species of rays, less than one-third have barbs (stinging spines). Barbless rays are those like the devil rays, sawfish, shovelnose rays, and the 'shark-like' rays, including the 'shark ray' (how's that for a confusing name!). Electric rays, including numbfish, don't have barbs, either. Instead, they actively stun their prey using electricity that they make themselves! What an awesome bunch of animals!

Rays are closely related to sharks, but there are some notable differences. When distinguishing between the two groups, rays are generally the flat ones, although some sharks, like wobbegongs and angel sharks, are flat, too. Rays have spiracles (which some species use for sucking in water) on top of their heads, and their gills are always on the underside of their body. Shark spiracles and gills, on the other hand, are always on the sides of their body. Most sharks use a side-to-side tail movement to push them through the water, whereas most (but not all!) rays 'flap' their wings up and down.

WATER HOLES AND DEATH ROLLS

The gigantic Mesozoic plesiosaurs, mosasaurs and ichthyosaurs are long gone. However, giant marine reptiles still swim in our oceans! These include the legendary saltwater crocodiles. Saltwater crocodiles, or 'salties', are the largest of all crocodilians, and they are serious predators! Unlike most other dangerous marine animals, saltwater crocodiles naturally live in the same environments as humans.

Despite their big, bulky appearance, saltwater crocodiles are actually creatures of stealth. Crocodiles can stay completely still, allowing them to blend in with their muddy or grassy surroundings. They can also float almost completely motionless in water, with most of their body submerged. But, by keeping their noses, eyes and just the tippy-tops of their heads above the surface, they can maintain their stealthy manoeuvres while still maximising the use of their exceptional sensory abilities. Crocodiles can also sit and wait patiently on the bottom of the water, completely submerged, for a few hours. This allows them to wait for and stalk unsuspecting prey near the surface, completely masked by murky water.

Saltwater crocodiles have quite characteristic short, but dramatic methods of attack. Generally, salties will stalk their prey, then lunge, using their incredibly powerful tail, before taking their prey through a 'death roll'. Finally, they submerge underwater with the unlucky victim. Crocodiles can move quickly on land when they want to, reaching speeds of over 10 kilometres per hour. However, they are most deadly while in the water. Although they look like they are just lazily floating along, crocodiles can attack from the water in a fraction of a second! In these instances, they can launch themselves at more than 40 kilometres per hour!

Crocodiles are opportunistic predators, and they will eat fish, birds, kangaroos, pigs and dogs. They sometimes even target much larger animals, like cows or horses that come to drink at a river's edge or water hole. Once something is in a crocodile's super-powerful jaws, there is little chance of escape. Crocodiles don't chew, they simply bite and swallow small prey. When tackling larger animals, they bite and then violently shake their heads and roll around until they break the animal into bite-sized pieces. Crocodiles sometimes even store parts of their kill under logs for later!

Despite their huge size, saltwater crocodiles rely on stealth for catching their meals.

Shark vs croc

Who would win between a shark and a crocodile? Crocodiles and some species of sharks (like bull sharks and river sharks) do share the same environments, so this battle for 'king (or queen) of the river' does sometimes occur! Sharks and crocs are both incredible predators – and also incredibly well defended – so the outcome would ultimately come down to the size, strength and stealth of the two animals involved. If all else was equal, either could win!

How do you avoid being on a croc's menu? Well, the best way is to be careful around waterways where crocodiles live. If you absolutely need to be by the water, you can throw rocks into the water at short intervals to test the area – just make sure you stand far back while doing so! Otherwise, if the water is clear, someone can act as a lookout. Or, you could watch for the movement of plants in the water, suggesting something is dragging these from below. But essentially, just staying well away from any water's edge (including beaches, riverbanks and billabongs) in places where crocodiles are known to live is the best idea!

SMALL(ER), BUT DEADLY(ER)

The marine world shows us very clearly that size does not necessarily equate to deadliness. In fact, despite the massive difference in size, power and number of teeth, jellyfish cause more serious and fatal injuries to humans than sharks. The biggest gelatinous culprits are the approximately 50 species of Cubozoans, or box jellyfish, that inhabit tropical and temperate oceans around the globe. The Australian box jellyfish is often considered to be *the* most venomous marine animal. The tentacles of these jellies can be up to 3 metres long, and they are covered with hundreds of thousands of specialised stinging cells. Paralysis, heart failure and death can occur in humans within minutes of being stung by one of these not-to-be-messed-with animals.

Not only are box jellyfish extremely venomous but they are capable of swimming – and quite quickly at that. They can travel at speeds of up to 7 kilometres per hour! Strangely, they also have a set of 24 eyes – six of each in four different types: upper

Eyes up

The upper lens eyes of box jellyfish are suspended within the animal's body. No matter what position the jellyfish is in, these eyes rotate around so that they are always pointing up towards the water's surface. Creepy … but beneficial! The water in the preferred environment of these jellies – mangrove lagoons – is often too murky to see in. So, instead, they use their always-upward facing eyes to navigate using terrestrial structures, like mangrove branches, and the light from the sky.

and lower lens eyes, pit eyes and slit eyes. Some of these eyes are complex enough to be structurally similar to vertebrate eyes. As such, it's almost a bit of a letdown that their visual capacity only extends to sensing light and dark! Still, this is enough to allow them to navigate to preferred habitats, avoid objects and vary their swim speed in line with whatever mission they are on.

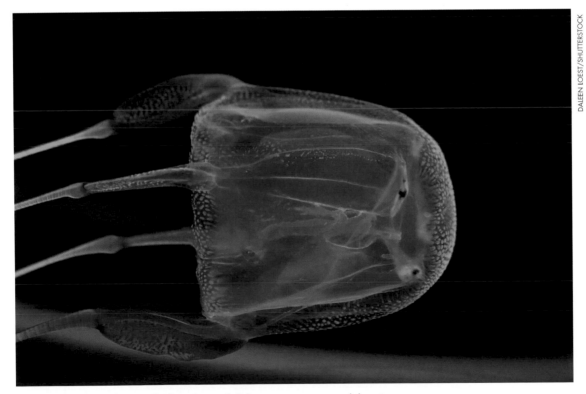

It's worth getting to know all about box jellyfish – so you can avoid them!

Chapter 9

BFFs

There is no-one like your bestie. They're the one person you know you can count on when things get rough. And, more than anyone else, you know they've got your back. While 'friendship' is a human thing and not a term that we often use for animal relationships, some animals are certainly capable of forming strong social bonds. Others are completely reliant on one another and may even, quite literally, stick together, no matter what life throws at them!

SAFETY IN NUMBERS

Life is full of challenges for sea turtles, and these challenges start early! Newly hatched sea turtles have to do a dangerous dash across the sand from their nest to the sea. Turtle hatching is a big event on the marine world calendar, and many other animals come for the party. Unfortunately, they are not there to welcome the new babies to the big, wide

Blinded by the light

One of the biggest threats to baby turtles is light pollution. Baby turtles rely on the moonlight reflecting off the water to get to the sea, so lights on land can cause them to head the wrong way!

world; instead, they show up in the hope of a shelled snack. To help their odds, baby turtles will often all leave the nest at the same time. For example, setting off together allows about 90% of loggerhead turtle babies to make it safely from the nest to the water.

Life is hard when you are a baby sea turtle! Luckily, your brothers and sisters are there to create safety in numbers.

Sea-lebrities
SEA TURTLES

BLAKE CHAPMAN

Sea turtles are not built for life on land, so the process of nesting in the soft sand above the high-water mark is exhausting work!

There are seven species of sea (or marine) turtles: flatback, leatherback, green, hawksbill, Kemp's ridley, loggerhead and olive ridley. Leatherbacks are the largest of the group: their shells can measure more than 2 metres in length, and they can weigh up to 650 kilograms!

Pregnant sea turtles often return to the same place they were born to lay their own eggs. They push through crashing surf and drag their large bodies over the soft sand until they are well past the reach of the biggest and highest tides. There, they dig a nest with their back flippers, then lay their eggs. The whole process can take up to 3 hours! Exhausted, the turtles drag themselves back to the ocean.

Sea turtles worldwide are in trouble due to climate change. Rising sea levels could cause havoc to sea turtles if it means that they can no longer return to the nesting sites they know and rely on. Also, remarkably, the temperature of the sand determines the gender of sea turtles: cooler sand produces more males, and warmer sand produces more females. Experts are concerned that warmer temperatures across the globe could lead to too many female sea turtles and not enough males, which could be bad news for populations overall.

We humans are failing sea turtles in other ways, too. They are getting tangled in our fishing gear, and too much of our rubbish is ending up in the oceans. Turtles are mistaking our trash for their food. Unfortunately, this can be a fatal mistake.

Light pollution confuses turtles

Buildings and other changes to nesting beaches can make it difficult for females to lay eggs

STORI

Increased air temperature affects nesting habitat and hatchling gender

Pets and feral animals (like cats and rats) dig up turtle eggs

Plastic debris can be eaten by turtles, leading to illness or even death

Fishing nets and gear can injure and drown turtles

CLOWNING AROUND

One of the best-known relationships in the marine world is between clownfish and anemones. These animals aren't friends, though. Instead, they have more of an *'I'll help you, you help me'* relationship. This is called **symbiosis**. Symbiosis is where two or more organisms work together to achieve common goals – like survival! Or, in some cases, one might get something out of the relationship while the other just gets on with its life, neither helped nor harmed by the tag-along.

Anemones and clownfish need each other. In fact, some of these species can't survive without each other; they are called **obligate symbionts**. This relationship is so critical that clownfish are more commonly known as anemonefish. Anemones (pronounced AH-nem-oh-NEEs) are predatory marine animals related to corals and jellyfish. Most anemones stick tight to rocks or other hard surfaces whereas others hold fast to sandy substrates. In many ways, anemones look like small trees. They have a trunk, but instead of leaves, they are topped with a disc of stinging tentacles.

BLAKE CHAPMAN

Anemones and anemonefish are perfect together.

Anemonefish take up residence within the tentacles of anemones. But what about the stinging? Amazingly, the anemone stinging cells that can kill other small marine animals do not harm anemonefish. How, you might wonder? It's all thanks to a special protective mucous coat. That's right … a snot coat. These fish are safe and right-at-home within the hostile tentacles of the anemone. Predators trying to get to the fish, however, are zapped by the anemone. They may be clownfish, but they do not make a happy meal – at least not when defended by an anemone!

Anemonefish wisdom: keep your friends close and your anemones closer!

Sea-ing stars

Sea stars are sometimes called starfish. But since they are not fish – they are echinoderms, like urchins and sea cucumbers – sea star is the correct name. Sea stars crawl over their prey or use their arms to wrap themselves around it. Then they eat. In some cases, this involves them pushing their stomach outside of their body to digest their food directly. Gross … but you can't fault their efficiency!

Anemonefish help out their anemone, as well. They chase away would-be anemone-munchers, like butterflyfish (which only pick at anemones, allowing them to avoid major stings), snails, sea slugs and sea stars. They also finish anemones' leftovers, helping to keep them clean. Anemones are pretty helpless when it comes to creating water flow, so when things get still, the fish get moving. This artificially increases water flow through the tentacles, bringing with it oxygen and nutrients. Oh, and just when you thought this unlikely pair couldn't be any more bonded – anemones also appear to score essential nutrients from anemonefish pee (and other forms of fish waste)!

The relationship between this unlikely duo is so effective that anemonefish that are symbiotic with anemones live for an extraordinarily long time – around 30 years for the clownfish. Closely related fish that don't have symbiotic relationships with anemones tend to only live for half that long, and other similarly-sized fish usually only live one-sixth as long!

COMPULSIVE CLEANERS … AND CHEATERS

Cleaner wrasse are certainly some of the most popular fish on the reef. These awesome little fish set up areas known as 'cleaning stations'. Cleaning stations generally consist of one male, and one or two females. Cleaner wrasse service a wide variety of 'clients' – most of which are much larger than them, and many of whom would, in other circumstances, prefer them as a snack. Typical cleaner clients are fish, sharks, rays and turtles, but cleaner wrasse also clean crocodiles, marine iguanas and marine mammals!

Bleached views

You may have heard of coral bleaching, but did you know it's not just coral that can bleach? This alarmingly negative result of global warming can affect any animal that relies on symbiotic relationships with algae (called **zooxanthellae**), like corals, but also anemones. And although anemonefish are technically free-swimming animals capable of moving to where they need to be, their strong ties to their anemone keeps them close to home. As a result, they too are heavily affected by localised changes to the environment. Major bleaching events can result in large numbers of dead anemones and even local extinctions of anemonefish.

Anemonefish aren't the only animals that rely on symbiotic relationships with anemones. This fragile porcelain anemone crab also calls anemones home.

DENICE ASKEBRINK

'Oo I 'ave som-fing in my teef?' This lucky eel is being cleaned by both a cleaner wrasse (the blue fish) and a cleaner shrimp!

Clients swim up to a cleaner's station, stop completely (or as completely as possible), open their mouth, spread their fins and flare their gills. The cleaners then swim through every nook and cranny and clean it all. Even the teeth! Despite what would surely be a temptation, clients rarely eat the wrasse. Why? Because they offer a great service! Their cleaning service includes picking off parasites and removing dead or unhealthy bits of the animal. Parasites can be extremely uncomfortable and can cause extensive damage to fish: they can even lead to death!

In return, cleaner fish get to eat their finds. Even better, the food is brought straight to them – no tiresome searching or chasing required! Cleaner wrasse can eat more than 1200 parasites a day, and some fish visit their local cleaning station up to 100 times a day!

But things are not as perfect as they may seem ... Cleaner wrasse have a naughty secret: they prefer to eat the client's mucus and scales. Scandalous! In the cleaning biz, this is considered cheating. Cheated-on clients may lash out by aggressively chasing the cleaner or boycotting their station, opting to visit another cleaner instead. Or, the client could eat the cleaner! It's risky business – if the cleaner gets away with it, the client only loses – at most – a bit of flesh. Sorry, not sorry! But if not, the wrasse could lose its life!

'I'm just gonna lay here and let you clean me ...'

What's even more entertaining about these cheeky little reef fish is that they have learned to use touch as a positive social behaviour. Touching a client's dorsal fins with their pelvic and pectoral fins lowers stress in their clients and allows the cleaners to build good relationships with them. This is especially handy for winning new clients. Cleaners that have been caught cheating will offer extra touches as a cheeky apology – just like when humans offer flowers as a way to make up for their bad behaviour!

Cleaners who plan to cheat (yes, they even plan this behaviour in advance!) spend an extra amount of time touching clients before doing the deed. They also give a bit of extra attention to predatory species that could, if they wanted to, turn around and eat them. It all sounds like a dramatically scripted marine soap opera! But overall, it shows that these clever cleaners are capable of social manipulation (like bribing), pre-conflict management (extra touches when they intend to be naughty), and reconciliation (more touches afterwards).

Mimicry is the best form of flattery

Cleaner wrasse have such a good gig and are so trusted within their community that other species, like the false cleaner fish, have copied the cleaners' body colouration and patterns. These look-alike mimics don't clean themselves, but use the reputation of cleaner wrasse to get close enough to other fish so that they can take a bite. This is bad news for business, though! Cleaner wrasse are very territorial and always set up shop in the same place, so clients get to know their cleaners. If a mimic bites in a cleaners' territory, clients – not recognising the difference in the two fish – may lose faith in their local cleaning station and go somewhere else.

OPPOSITES ATTRACT

Groupers and moray eels could not be more different to each other! Groupers are large, football-shaped fish with big heads. They normally hunt during the day, in open water where their size and body shape are not a problem. Giant moray eels, on the other hand, are long and thin. They are generally active at night, when they weave their bodies through rocks and tight crevices.

Differences aside, these fish have developed extremely cool cooperative behaviours that increase their chances of catching a meal. And it's because of how different these fish are that they work so well together. Groupers' prey often escapes by seeking cover in rocks or coral, whereas morays' prey tends to escape into open water. See where this is going? The fish certainly do!

Incredibly, these two completely different, unrelated species have developed a way of communicating with each other. Groupers will actively seek out morays and get nice and close. They then start shaking their head really fast, indicating *Come on! Come on! I'm HUNGRY!!*. This signal is effective in luring a resting moray from its slumber more than half the time. The two fish then swim off together for hunts that can last as long as 45 minutes. Search for the *Nature* video 'grouper and moray hunting' online to see this unexpected but extraordinary behaviour!

Groupers can be very compelling when they're hungry, attracting even snoozing morays for hunting outings.

Morays can wiggle their way into the tiniest of nooks.

If a yummy morsel swims past and into a tight spot, a solo grouper may even seek out a nearby moray. Groupers perform a slightly different shimmy to tell the moray *'Come now, I SAW something!',* then lead their sidekick straight to the hidden prey.

The coordinated efforts between the grouper and moray create an attack that is difficult for prey to escape. Even though the grouper and eel don't share their catches – it's always a polite winner-takes-all scenario – both are more successful in their attempts overall. Groupers with morays are more than five times as likely to come away with a full belly, compared to when they hunt alone! Morays are also clearly far more successful with this strategy since they deem it worth waking up for. Remarkably, the pairs never fight.

STUCK ON YOU

We all have people that we love to be around. But how would you feel if you were stuck with your special someone, day-in and day-out. And by stuck, I don't just mean that they always *seem* to be around – I mean *stuck* stuck. They *are* always there. This is the reality for the deep-sea fanfin anglerfish.

The deep sea would be a big, vast, seemingly empty place. There's no light, lots of open space, some truly bizarre and scary animals randomly popping up, and no Netflix! So yes, you might be happy for a lifelong mate that you knew would always be there for you. That is what the fanfin angler specialises in. The female fanfin is elaborate and beautiful (well, depending on your standards, I guess). She's got lovely lumpy, bumpy skin, beautiful bulges, beady little eyes, long gnarly teeth and a lovely array of long, threadlike **finrays**. She also has an alluring bioluminescent lure that dangles off the front of her head. Then there's the male.

Male deep-sea anglerfish are less spectacular. They're also tiny. In some of the more extreme deep-sea anglerfish species, the male is 60 times smaller than the female and roughly *half a million times* lighter! Can you imagine approaching a potential mate 60 times your size and asking to tag along? Luckily for the males, they, as well as their potential partners, have an excellent sense of smell that allows them to recognise each other. This saves a lot of awkward *'oops, I accidentally ate my mate'* moments.

As male fanfin anglerfish mature, they lose their teeth. These are replaced by a set of pincer-like bones right at the front of their jaw. This way, when they do find that special someone, they can perform a stalkerish grip-on-and-hold-fast manoeuvre! Then – get this – the male will actually fuse to the female. He becomes entirely reliant on her and will go so far as to tap into her bloodstream. This provides him with all of the good stuff in life – nutrients, oxygen and hormones. What more could he ask for?

FANFIN ANGLERFISH

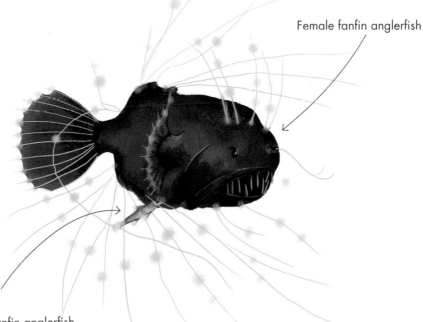

Female fanfin anglerfish

Attached male fanfin anglerfish

The name game

It is commonly known that a group of fish is called a school. But there are some other fun names for groups of marine animals. A group of jellyfish is called a smack, dugongs come together in herds, dolphins travel in pods, a group of stingrays is called a fever, and you could come across a cast of crabs while looking through a colony of coral!

Sometimes the female carries the male around at the end of a long stalk (weird!), while in other species, the male is kept so close that his head gets absorbed by the female (creepy!). Clearly, in the fanfin world, having a head is overrated, anyway. The male gets a free ride, free food, blood, etc. The female, well, she gets to have babies whenever she wants. While there might be lots of fish in the sea, the right fish can be hard to find. This especially holds true in the deep sea. That is … unless he's attached to you!

You *have* to see this for yourself – search online for 'First footage of deep-sea anglerfish pair'. Beasty besties, or just plain disturbing? I'll let you decide!

Cownose rays come together in large groups to migrate, creating an absolutely stunning (and hypnotic) sight!

NSW DEPARTMENT OF PRIMARY INDUSTRIES/SOUTHERN CROSS UNIVERSITY

Sea 'smarts'

What do animals know? Are they smart, dumb, or somewhere in between? These are important questions – but complicated.

When brainstorming animal brainpower, we have to be careful not to let our 'humanness' influence our thoughts. Humans are oddballs! That is, at least, in comparison to other animals. No other animal comes close to us in terms of intelligence or social complexity. However, ironically, intelligence is a tricky thing to understand. What makes something intelligent, and how do you even define animal smarts? We often think people who do really well in school are smart. And, of course, they are. But that's not the only way to measure intelligence. Important signs of intelligence in the animal world are things like being able to solve problems and form complex relationships – and really, just being able to survive!

TOOL TIME

Dolphins are generally considered to be the smartest of marine animals. One way they demonstrate this is through the range of tactics they use to find and catch their food. Sometimes, they even use tools! Some dolphins hunt by digging around in the seagrass and sandy substrate. This is known as 'bottom grubbing'. But while doing so, they can get scratched by rocks or sharp pieces of shells. To fix this, a select group of bottlenose dolphins in Shark Bay, Australia uses marine basket sponges for protection. They break off a chunk of the sponge and carry it in their mouths while they dig! This clever strategy is known as 'sponge foraging', or 'sponging'.

Dolphins are excellent echolocators, and they also have good vision – so why would they bother digging in the sand for food, risking injury? Well, possibly because prey that don't have swim bladders (an organ many fish have to help them float) are not as easily picked up by echolocation, and buried prey can be difficult to see. This alternate method of foraging allows these particular dolphins to access a different food source to the other dolphins, meaning there is less competition for food. It's

AILIE SUZUKI

There is nothing common about how smart common dolphins are!

Sea-lebrities
SPONGES

Talk about 'been there, done that' – marine sponges are among the oldest known multicellular organisms. They first appeared more than 500 million years ago!

Although some super-smart dolphins have learned to use sponges as tools for hunting, sponges themselves may not be the best example of extreme intelligence. After all, these simple, immobile, filter-feeding animals don't have any internal organs, muscles, a nervous system or a circulatory system! However, they do still have some 'smart' tricks up their pores.

There are more than 8000 species of sponges known, and probably close to that many more yet to be discovered. Sponges are extremely diverse and come in a wide variety of colours, shapes and sizes. They range from 1 centimetre to 2 metres high, and they can be 1.5 metres wide!

Marine sponges are found across the world's oceans in shallow and deep water, from the tropics to the polar oceans. Sponges are full of holes that allow water to move through them. And, like the sponges we are more familiar with, marine sponges also take up large quantities of water. In nature, they do this to filter bacteria, plankton and dissolved food from the water.

Sponges can release toxic substances into the environment. Other animals move away, allowing the sponge to claim the 'best spot on the block'. Sponges are also great at defending themselves against foreign attackers, like viruses and bacteria. Because of that, they have sparked a lot of interest in medicine. Scientists believe that these simple organisms may be able to give us the upper hand against some nasty bacterial, viral, fungal and parasitic diseases!

It's all fun and brains

Brainy animals, like dolphins, sea otters and polar bears are known to play with things that they find in their environment, like shells, seagrass or even pieces of plastic. Dolphins, for example, have been observed playing 'keep-away'. When a game is done, they may swallow the 'toy', only to bring it back up later for the next game. Dolphins may be known for their intelligence, but this is definitely not something to learn from them!

a win-win all around! Except for the prey. They tend to lose to these 'tool-rific' dolphins. Using sponges to extract hard-to-locate but highly nutritious food (no air-filled swim bladder = more fishy goodness per bite) is a great example of problem-solving. And being able to solve problems is a great answer to the question of what makes something smart!

Dolphins also show intelligence through complex social relationships. In fact, these animals come as close to having friends as possible, without actually being scientifically termed 'friends'. Male bottlenose dolphins often have two besties that they prefer to go about their daily business with. They help each other to find girls, and they have each other's back when trying to win over girls from other groups. These tight bro-bonds can last 20 years or more.

AILIE SUZUKI

Dolphins are extremely social animals, and they learn from each other. What do you think this Hector's dolphin is teaching her bub?

GABRIEL BARATHIEU

Sperm whales form close relationships within small units, but also mix with other animals in their clan.

Sperm whales are truly unique animals. They're the largest of the toothed whales, and they are wrinklier than your grandparents after a long bath. And strangely, their blowhole (yes, I said blowhole) is noticeably skewed to the left. They are dark brownish-grey and have a stumpy dorsal fin and smallish pectoral fins. But what they lack in fin, they make up for in forehead! Their enormous, square head can make up as much as a third of their body length. Sperm whales fill their huge heads with huge brains. In fact, the sperm whale brain is the largest of any living animal – it is even 60% larger than an elephant's brain.

One of the advantages of extra-large brains is a great capacity for social behaviour and communication. Sperm whales form long-term social 'units' that usually contain around 10–12 often-related females and their immature offspring. But these animals also form much larger 'clans' that span thousands of kilometres and include thousands of animals. Clans transmit their culture through their chatter. Sperm whale culture influences everything from their social structure to movement patterns. Culture may even be more important than how closely related the animals are to each other.

Sperm whales are found throughout the world's oceans. They are mammals, and therefore breathe air, so they need to spend some time at the surface. But they are also designed to go deep! Sperm whales can dive to depths of over 2000 metres to hunt their favourite food.

Like dolphins and orcas, sperm whales also use echolocation. They produce clicks by pushing air through their enormous forehead. These clicks are thought to be the loudest sound produced by any animal. The fact that their favourite food – bioluminescent squid – is known for its ability to light up, however, suggests that they also rely on vision. Having really effective ways of finding food would be crucial for sperm whales since they need to eat *1 tonne of food per day!* It's hard to even imagine that much squid!

SMART SUCKERS

Octopuses are awesome! They have one beak, three hearts and eight arms covered in big, strong suckers. They have blue blood (because theirs is based on copper, while our red blood is based on iron), they can shoot ink, and they've got some serious sea smarts. And, like dolphins, they use tools. This might not sound like an incredible feat, but only because we are biased from being so smart ourselves. In fact, for a long time it was believed that only humans were smart enough to use tools – the skill is that special and unusual. We now know that we're not alone in this ability, but only a few other super-smart animals, like chimpanzees, dolphins, octopuses and crows, have the intelligence to do this. What's even more impressive is that these animals don't just use tools, they also make decisions around if and when to use tools, and exactly which tools to use!

Tool use in the octopus world doesn't mean picking up a hammer and knocking out a house. Instead, they do things like gather discarded coconut shells and carry them around as a pre-made house. These make-shift mobile homes provide them with protection when needed. After all, octopuses are soft and squishy, and a preferred prey item of many animals. Coconut shells, on the other hand, are generally unappealing, inedible and strong. They are so strong that they have even been proposed as a natural additive into concrete. Having this sort of protection on-tentacle is a smart idea! Want to see them doing this for yourself? Search 'octopus using coconut shell' online.

Other octopuses do actually build homes for themselves. Some choose sheltered areas among rocky reefs, but others build dens with empty mollusc shells from past meals. Octopuses may even go so far as to use rocks or sponges to close off the entrance to their den. Although these animals usually prefer their own company,

Octopuses are clever enough to use tools, like empty shells, for hiding and protection.

ironically large numbers of gloomy octopus (yes, that is their real name!) have been found living close to each other. At these sites, the octopuses live in dens made from empty scallop shells. But the closeness of these living arrangements often becomes *too* close for comfort. The behaviours between neighbouring octopuses are complex – lots of signalling, mating, defence manoeuvres, evictions and the exclusion of particular animals. It all sounds more dramatic than reality TV!

Octopuses kept in aquariums continuously wow visitors and staff with their cheeky intelligence. They open jars and even child-proof bottles to get to food treats. Clever! But their antics don't stop there. These eight-armed animals are also great escape artists. They have no bones, so they can fit through the smallest of gaps. There are reports of them sneakily escaping their own tank, only to visit a neighbouring one, snag a snack, and then return to their home tank. They do this all without a trace of their deed ... apart from the missing snack-sized neighbour!

KEY INTELLIGENCE

Sea otters are admittedly super-cute, but they are also super-smart. They, too, use tools in a variety of ways. Otters may use rocks or stones to pluck mussel or abalone shells off rocks. Or, they might use rocks to pry or hammer shells open to get into the fleshy food inside. When the job is done, they store their favourite tools in 'pockets' made from the loose skin folds of their armpits – ready for next time!

The sea otter tool-chest (or maybe tool-pit!) is not limited to rocks and stones. They also use kelp! Some otters wrap captured crabs in kelp to prevent them from scampering away while they continue to hunt or eat other food. In other situations, otters may also wrap themselves in kelp. This helps to prevent them from drifting away while they drift-off for a snooze. The buoyant kelp also helps to keep otters afloat.

Sea otters eat a variety of different foods, such as crabs, sea urchins, snails and abalone. However, individuals have strong preferences for certain foods. One otter might looooove kelp crabs, for example, whereas the next one over may never eat a kelp crab. Instead, that one might live almost entirely off turban snails.

Table manners

Sea otters often hunt on the sea floor, but they always return to the surface to eat. They eat floating on their back, using their chest as a table!

Sea otters are what is known as a **keystone species**. This means they have an extra-important role in keeping their environment – in their case, near-shore kelp forests – in balance. Kelp forests are important for providing cover and food for many marine animals. But because these ecosystems are based on something as fragile as living

MIKE BAIRD

As with dolphins, only certain sea otters use tools for foraging. Interestingly, both food preferences and tool use are passed from mum to bub.

Fuzzy-wuzzy

Unlike other marine mammals, sea otters don't have blubber to keep them warm. Instead, they have incredibly dense fur, with as many as 120 000–140 000 hairs per square centimetre. Their hair is critical to their survival, so it is not surprising that they spend a great deal of time keeping it in tip-top condition!

kelp, they are far less stable than those based on rock, or even coral. Kelp forests can quite easily appear and disappear as a result of changes in ocean conditions, like weather, swell and nutrient load. One critical factor is the presence of animals that eat kelp – for example, sea urchins. Sea urchins can move through kelp forests in large herds and their numbers can quickly become out of control. Enter: the otters! Sea otters save the day by loving to eat the animals that love to eat kelp.

CLINT CHAPMAN

Otters will often join together in 'rafts'.

Dive in and create waves of change!

~~~~~

THE GREAT UNKNOWN

Here's what we know: ocean animals are truly awesome! But what don't we know? Most likely, LOTS! It is thought that less than 20% of the ocean has been explored. This is mind-blowing, but also *so* exciting to think about! Our knowledge of the marine world is so incomplete that we still don't even know if there are one million marine animal species or 10 million. When scientists explore the depths of the oceans, they sometimes find as many as 28 new species per dive!

Unfortunately, though, there are scary consequences of our lack of information. For example, with all of the major changes our planet is going through due to things like climate change and overfishing, we are running the risk of losing species to extinction before we've even realised that they're there. Another major issue is that the oceans are becoming more acidic due to the unnaturally high levels of carbon dioxide we are pumping into the atmosphere. Carbon dioxide is produced by human activities like burning fuels for electricity and transportation. The increased acidity is having some really strange effects on marine animals. In lab tests, one fish species raised in the anticipated ocean conditions of the near future lost the inborn – and crucial – ability to recognise predators. Instead of avoiding them, these fish were strongly attracted to predators!

GET YOUR HANDS WET

Most of us don't have the opportunity to jump into a deep-sea submersible and head off on a discovery mission. But that shouldn't stop us from doing what we can to explore, learn and gain hands-on knowledge of our favourite marine animals. I have a few tips for getting up-close and personal with animals of the watery world. So finish these last few pages, grab your binoculars, magnifying glass, camera, mask and snorkel (if you really want to dive in head-first), and get out there! Oh, don't forget to grab a parent, too!

My first tip is: start your research before you go. Some things, like tide times, change every day, though, so make sure you make a plan for the exact day you expect to go. Low tide is usually best – especially if you are visiting a beach with rock pools – since some exciting finds might not be exposed at high tide. It's also a good idea to do a bit of investigation on the area you'll be investigating. Knowing what animals you might come across will help you to not only know what to *look* for – but also what to *look out* for!

Another fun thing to do is find or download a species list or app for your preferred location or environment so that you can better identify, and also keep track of, what you see. You can always get your friends or classmates to do the same and see who can find the most – or most unique – animals!

If you're after a different experience that doesn't necessarily involve getting your feet wet or even sandy, you could visit a public aquarium. Aquariums display lots of animals from a variety of marine habitats, allowing you to get face-to-fin with animals that you may otherwise never get to see. Be sure to take a camera with you. Photographing animals in the water can be challenging – especially when they don't keep still – but it's also lots of fun. Plus, these photos leave you with great memories of your favourite finds that you can show off to your friends! Most aquariums have touch pools where you can get hands-on with marine animals (okay, so maybe you will choose to get a little wet). For the more adventurous, there are often animal encounters on offer, where you can get so close you can smell the squiddy-breath!

No matter where you go, though, whether it is the beach, rock pools, aquariums or the wide-open oceans, just be sure to always respect the animals and environments that you come in contact with. Make sure you don't take anything away or leave anything behind. Also, be sure to use extra caution when exploring rock pools – the rocks can be super-slippery, and tides can come in surprisingly quickly!

CLINT CHAPMAN

When exploring marine environments, remember you are in the splash zone! Unexpectedly large waves can also come in at any time.

MAKE WAVES ... OF CHANGE

Everyone has a part to play in protecting and looking after our planet and its oceans. Humans have done a lot of not-nice things to our planet. As a result, the oceans and many of the animals living within them are struggling in one way or another.

Some of the main challenges our marine animals are facing come from climate change. While the changes – in terms of the number of degrees that the oceans are warming – may look small, they are a big deal! Other big problems challenging our oceans and marine animals are the major accumulation of nasty plastics, other pollution, the destruction of natural habitats for buildings and infrastructure and the introduction of **invasive species**. Invasive species can really disrupt ecosystems and cause catastrophic changes to important native populations.

Want to lend a helping hand to the oceans? There are lots of things you can do! Some of the easiest but most powerful actions are:

- Say no to unnecessary single-use plastics, like straws and balloons.

- Use reusable water bottles and food containers – all day, every day.

- Look, but don't disturb natural habitats or remove any animals from their environment.

- Make sure all of your rubbish ends up in the bin. If it's safe to do so, pick up any other rubbish you see lying around when you're out and about.

- Reduce, reuse and recycle! Be creative – there is *so* much you can do in this space!

- Switch off lights and devices that plug in whenever you're not using them.

- Encourage your family to walk or take public transport instead of driving.

- Encourage your parents to buy only sustainably fished seafood.

- Participate in beach clean-ups.

- Keep domestic pets domestic – don't let them wander about where they could disrupt or harm natural environments or native animals.

- Fall in love with the natural environment ... and share the love!

Hey, no snoozing … it's time to get up and explore the marine world!

And finally, if you really want to create change, consider becoming a **citizen scientist** or environmental advocate! Never feel that you are too small to make a big difference or that the actions of one person won't matter. Sometimes, the littlest people make the biggest difference! Through her 'Straw No More' campaign, a 10-year-old girl in Cairns, Australia was able to convince the local Regional Council (which notably governs the land closest to the Great Barrier Reef) to work towards completely eliminating plastic straws. What a champion! There are lots of citizen science programs out there, too, so there's sure to be one that sparks your interest. One great example is an app called QuestaGame.

QuestaGame encourages you to seek and find wild animals. Your mission is to photograph and log as many new plant and animal species as possible. You can win game-gold for each species and compete against other players from around the world

The lesson from these baby green turtles is that the path isn't always easy, but finding your way to the water's edge is a great first step!

to see who can find the most animals. The best part is that the info you collect is shared with biodiversity databases, and real scientists can access your sightings to study the animals you've found. This helps them to track where animals are living. New species have even been identified by photos that citizen scientists (like yourself) have logged!

So, there is only question left: how will you choose to make a difference in protecting and conserving our incredible marine animals?

Marine phyla

The animals discussed in the book are listed here. They are grouped taxonomically, by the most general categories of **Phylum** and **Class** (where possible). The taxonomic system of classification is a scientific way of grouping living things based on how similar they are in their design and development and how closely they are related to each other.

The taxonomic categories of animals are (from most generic to most specific):

KINGDOM (all animals are in the Kingdom Animalia)

Phylum

Class

Order

Family

Genus

Species

For example, the nervous shark, which is scientifically known as *Carcharhinus cautus*, is taxonomically classified as:

KINGDOM: Animalia (it is an animal)

PHYLUM: Chordata (it has features such as both sides of its body being symmetrical and it has a notochord and a dorsal nerve cord)

CLASS: Chondrichthyes (it is a jawed vertebrate with a skeleton made of cartilage; it also has paired fins and scales, among other defining characteristics)

ORDER: Carcharhiniformes (it is a member of the largest group of shark species, the 'ground sharks'; it has two dorsal fins, an anal fin and a lower eyelid called a nictitating membrane)

FAMILY: Carcharhinidae (it is a 'requiem shark'; its mouth is on the underside of its body, it has two spineless dorsal fins, five gill slits, and gives birth to live young, among other distinctive characteristics)

GENUS: *Carcharhinus* (its first dorsal fin does not have substantial black or white tips, its second dorsal fin is about half the height of the first, it has broad, triangular shaped upper teeth, etc)

SPECIES: *cautus* (its pectoral fins are not noticeably broad or triangular, it has black edging on the dorsal and caudal fins, etc)

You can see how with each level, the criteria get more detailed, so the number of animals in more specific categories would become fewer and fewer, until only one species fits all of the defining criteria.

Looking for a way to learn even more about marine animals? You could always look up the marine phyla that haven't been discussed in this book and find some amazing examples of them to tell your friends about!

Phylum Acanthocephala *(parasitic spiny-headed worms)*

Phylum Annelida *(segmented worms, includes tube worms, bristle worms and sand worms)*

   Class Polychaeta

      Christmas tree worm

      Giant tube worm

Phylum Arthropoda *(Arthropods: invertebrate crustaceans with segmented bodies and jointed limbs, including sea spiders, lobsters, crabs, barnacles and krill)*

   Class Hexanauplia

      Copepod

   Class Malacostraca

      Decorator crab

      Isopod

      Japanese spider crab

      Kelp crab

      Mantis shrimp

      Snapping shrimp

      Tongue biter

Phylum Brachiopoda *(sessile, filter-feeding bivalve molluscs called lamp shells)*

Phylum Chaetognatha *(arrow or glass worms)*

Phylum Chordata *(fish, mammals, birds, reptiles and amphibians)*

   Class Actinopterygii

      Anemonefish

      Bathysaurus

      Blackspot anglerfish

      Cleaner wrasse

      Clownfish

      Crocodile fish

      False cleanerfish

      Fanfin anglerfish

      Flying fish

      Giant moray eel

      Grouper

      Leaf scorpionfish

      Oarfish

      Ocean sunfish

      Pufferfish

      Sailfish

      Summer flounder

      Viperfish

   Class Aves

      Albatross

      Gentoo penguin

   Class Chondrichthyes

      Cookiecutter shark

      Goblin shark

      Grey nurse shark

      Hammerhead shark

      Nervous shark

      Port Jackson shark

      Sawfish

      Thresher shark

      White-spotted eagle ray

      White shark

   Class Hyperoartia

      Sea lamprey

   Class Mammalia

      Blue whale

      Common dolphin

      Dugong

      Elephant seal

      Hector's dolphin

      Manatee

      Orca whale

      Polar bear

      Sea otter

      Sperm whale

   Class Myxini

      Hagfish

   Class Reptilia

      Saltwater crocodile

      Sea snake

      Sea turtle

   Class Thaliacea

      Pyrosome

      Salp

      Tunicate

Phylum Cnidaria (*jellyfish, anemones and coral with stinging cells called nematocysts*)

> **Class Anthozoa**
>> Sea anemone
>
> **Class Cubozoa**
>> Box jellyfish
>
> **Class Scyphozoa**
>> Atolla jellyfish
>>
>> Lion's mane jellyfish
>>
>> Nomura's jellyfish

Phylum Ctenophora (*comb jellies and sea walnuts that lack stinging cells*)

Phylum Echinodermata (*Echinoderms: sea stars, sea cucumbers and sea urchins*)

> **Class Asteroidea**
>> Sea star
>
> **Class Echinoidea**
>> Flower urchin

Phylum Echiura (*spoon worms*)

Phylum Ectoprocta (*bryozoans*)

Phylum Entoprocta (*goblet worms*)

Phylum Gastrotricha (*microscopic hairybacks*)

Phylum Gnathostomulida (*microscopic ciliated jaw worms*)

Phylum Hemichordata (*acorn worms*)

Phylum Kinorhyncha (*microscopic invertebrates*)

Phylum Loricifera (*microscopic animals that do not have mitochondria and do not require oxygen to survive*)

Phylum Mollusca *Molluscs: sea snails, clams, octopus and squid*)

> **Class Cephalopoda**
>> Blue-ringed octopus
>>
>> Giant squid
>>
>> Gloomy octopus
>>
>> Nautilus
>
> **Class Gastropoda**
>> Cone snail
>>
>> Moon snail
>>
>> Sea hare
>>
>> Spanish dancer
>>
>> Turban snail

Phylum Nematoda (*roundworms and nematodes*)

Phylum Nemertea (*ribbon or proboscis worms*)

Phylum Phoronida (*horseshoe worms*)

Phylum Placozoa (*simple structured multicellular animals with flagella*)

Phylum Platyhelminthes (*unsegmented flatworms*)

Phylum Porifera (*invertebrate sponges*)

> Sponge

Phylum Priapulida (*priapulid worms*)

Phylum Sipuncula (*bilaterally symmetrical, unsegmented peanut worms*)

Phylum Tardigrada (*water bears*)

> Tardigrade

A solitary jellyfish silhouetted against a sea of blue.

Glossary

Abyssal The deep ocean

Acceleration The rate that something changes speed

Adaptation The process of change an organism goes through to become better suited to its environment and to increase its chance of survival

Apex predator An animal that takes rank at the very top of the food chain, having no natural predators

Appendage A body part that extends or projects off the body

Asymmetrical Having two sides that are not the same

Atmosphere The layer of gasses that surrounds the planet; most commonly known as 'air'

Bioluminescence The production and release of light by a living organism

Camouflage Colour or form that allow something to blend into its surroundings

Carnivore An animal that eats other animals

Cetacean A member of the order Cetacea, an entirely aquatic group of mammals that includes animals such as whales, dolphins and porpoises

Citizen scientist Someone who voluntarily takes part in scientific research activities and who does not necessarily have any formal qualifications

Class The fifth most specific category in the taxonomic classification of living things

Crustacean An arthropod invertebrate in the large and diverse class Crustacea that has a hard exoskeleton, or shell, covering its body; includes animals such as crabs, lobsters, prawns and barnacles

Dorsal fin An individual fin that originates on the back of an animal

Echinoderm An invertebrate animal in the phylum Echinodermata; includes animals such as sea stars, sea urchins and sea cucumbers

Echolocation The use of sound waves to identify the location and features of objects

Ecosystem A community of living organisms interacting with each other and the environment

Electroreception The detection of electrical fields or currents

Embryo An animal in the early stages of development that has not yet been born

Envenomation The process of venom being injected by bite or sting from a venomous animal

Exoskeleton A hard structure or skeleton on the *outside* of an animal's body that provides support and protection – in contrast to a skeleton that is found *inside* the body (endoskeleton), as in humans

Extinction The point where there are no living individuals of a particular species left; the dying out of a species

Family The third most specific category in the taxonomic classification of living things

Filter feeder An animal that feeds by straining suspended matter and food particles from the water

Finray The bony structures projecting from the skeleton that support the fins of fish

Food chain A way of relating organisms to each other based on what eats what. The top level apex animals, which have no natural predators, are at one end, and photosynthetic organisms are at the other end. Mesopredators, which both eat and are eaten by other animals, are in the middle

Fringing reef A coral reef that lies close to shore

Gastropod A mollusc in the large and diverse class Gastropoda; includes animals such as snails and whelks

Habitat The natural environment that an organism lives in, characterised by its physical and biological features

Herbivore An animal that eats plants

Introduced pest An animal that is not native to an area, and as a result of accidental or deliberate introduction, has a negative impact on the ecosystem

Invasive species A species that is not native to the ecosystem it is in, and is consequently likely to displace or cause harm to native species or the environment

Invertebrate An animal that does not have a backbone or bony skeleton

Keystone species A plant or animal that plays a unique or critical role in its ecosystem, and without which, the ecosystem would be dramatically different or even collapse

Larvae (Larval) The distinct and separate juvenile stage of an animal that occurs before it develops into an adult

Longline fishing A commercial fishing technique that uses numerous baited hooks that drop down at set intervals from a main line (which stays at the surface)

Mollusc An invertebrate animal in the phylum Mollusca, such as snails, mussels and squid, that have soft, unsegmented bodies, a muscular foot or tentacles, a head, and a mantle that can secrete a shell

Moult (Moulting) The shedding of external features of a body, like feathers, hair, skin or shell, to enable new growth

Nutrients Substances that come from food or the environment that are needed to allow a living thing to function

Obligate symbionts Organisms that work together and rely on each other for different aspects of survival

Order The fourth most specific category in the taxonomic classification of living things

Organism An individual plant, animal or single-celled life form; a living thing

Parasite An organism that lives in or on another organism (the host) and gets its food from or at the expense of its host

Pectoral fin Paired fins located on the sides of the body

Pelagic The open ocean; environments/inhabitants that live away from the shore and off the ocean floor

Pelvic fin Paired fins located on the underside of the body

Photosynthesis The biological process of using energy from sunlight to produce food and chemical energy

Phylum (Phyla) The second broadest level of classification for living things after kingdom; less specific than class

Phytoplankton Tiny drifting autotrophic (self-feeding) or photosynthetic organisms that produce their own food using energy from sunlight and give off oxygen as waste, such as algae

Pinniped 'Flipper-footed' marine mammals that have front and rear flippers, including animals such as seals, sea lions and walruses

Plankton The general name for any organism that cannot swim against the current

Poison A substance that can cause illness or death when ingested, inhaled or absorbed through the skin

Predator An animal that hunts, kills and eats other animals

Prey An animal that is hunted and killed by another animal for food; or, the act of hunting and eating another animal

Rostrum A snout or body part that extends outwards from the front of the head

Seamount An underwater mountain formed by volcanic activity

Sedentary Fixed in one place, often attached by its base; not mobile

Silhouette A featureless, solid image of something that lacks any detail other than its outline, usually seen because the object is directly in front of a light source

Substrate The base layer (the bottom), or a surface on which something lives or is attached

Symbiosis A relationship between two or more organisms that live or work closely together

Symmetrical Having two sides that are the same, or mirror images of each other

Terrestrial Dry land; an organism that lives on land

Toxin A poisonous substance that is produced by living cells or organisms

Trench A long, deep and often narrow channel in the ocean floor

Venom A naturally produced toxic substance that is injected by an animal by bite or sting and can cause harm or death

Vertebrate An animal with a backbone or spinal cord in the phylum Chordata and subphylum Vertebrata

Zooplankton Drifting or weakly swimming animals that need water currents to move long distances

Zooxanthellae Yellowish-brown photosynthetic algae that often live symbiotically with marine animals, such as corals and anemones